FLORIDA'S MANGROVES

FLORIDA'S MANGROVES

A Slightly Salty History

THOMAS KENNING

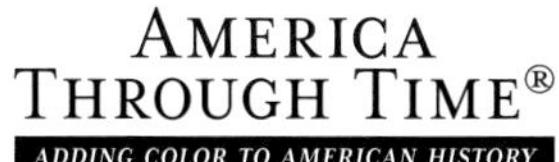

America Through Time is an imprint of Fonthill Media LLC
www.through-time.com
office@through-time.com

Published by Arcadia Publishing by arrangement with Fonthill Media LLC
For all general information, please contact Arcadia Publishing:
Telephone: 843-853-2070
Fax: 843-853-0044
E-mail: sales@arcadiapublishing.com
For customer service and orders:
Toll-Free 1-888-313-2665

www.arcadiapublishing.com

First published 2021

Copyright © Thomas Kenning 2021

ISBN 978-1-63499-349-4

Typeset in 10pt on 13pt Sabon
Printed and bound in England

CONTENTS

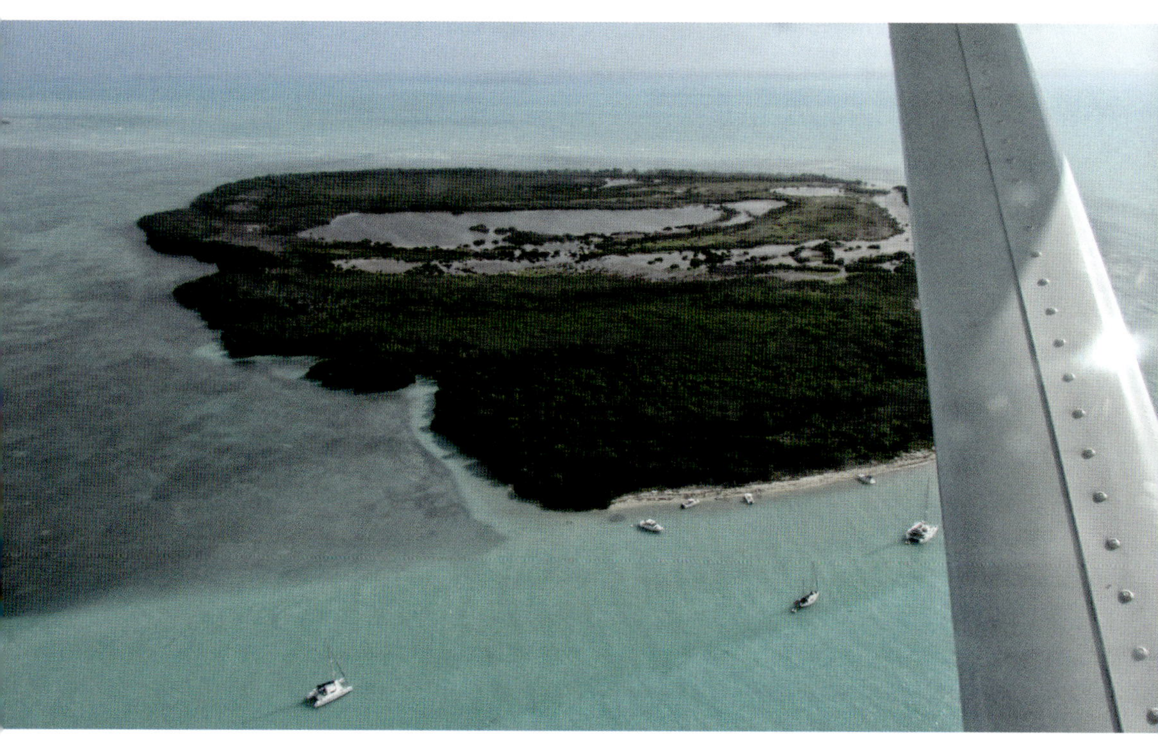

A small island in the Florida Strait, held together as many are by a forest of mangroves—as seen from the window of a DHC-3 Otter seaplane.

INTRODUCTION

For nothing is fixed, forever and forever and forever, it is not fixed; the earth is always shifting, the light is always changing, the sea does not cease to grind down rock. Generations do not cease to be born, and we are responsible to them because we are the only witnesses they have.
The sea rises, the light fails, lovers cling to each other, and children cling to us. The moment we cease to hold each other, the moment we break faith with one another, the sea engulfs us and the light goes out.

"Nothing Personal," James Baldwin, 1964

On a map or from high above, the Florida peninsula is little more than an unlikely spit of sand perched precariously between ocean and gulf. When the sea level rises just a few feet more, Florida's precious Everglades, its freshwater aquifers, and its many springs may all be inundated by salt—its lush green overtaken by sand, scrub, and saltwater marsh. A few more degrees of temperature, and the whole thing—most everything south of the panhandle's rolling hills—effectively slides under the waves.

For millions of years, in fact, this was the state of things—no dinosaur fossils will ever be found in Florida, because when those behemoths walked the Earth, the majority of the modern peninsula was underwater.

It is where things are headed once again, more or less.

Florida is an incredible balancing act between land and sea. This high wire routine is perhaps nowhere more visible than in the vast swathes of mangrove forest hugging the most sheltered portions of peninsular coastline—from Cedar Key on the Gulf Coast, down south through the Everglades and the Keys, sweeping north again on the Atlantic Coast, past Cape Canaveral. Incredibly sensitive to frost, but hardy enough to grow in salty, silty soil where no other broad-leafed tree can, Florida's mangroves congregate in the intertidal zones of bays, on the leeward edge of unassuming keys, in brackish estuaries—wherever the wave action is calm enough and the salinity amenable.

1

MANGROVE BASICS

The mangrove would make a good brand ambassador for the whole of Florida—an organism almost unique on the North American continent, languid and relaxed to an extreme, thriving in the salt air where others would wilt, and almost completely intolerant to the cold.

The term mangrove is a general one, referring to a range of trees and shrubs specially adapted to thrive in salty soil and water—a category of plants known by scientists as halophytes. They grow most anywhere slow-moving saline waters allow fine sediments to accumulate. There are more than fifty varieties of mangrove in the world, with the preponderance of that diversity centered in Southeast Asia.

In Florida, there are three unrelated species of mangrove occupying adjacent niches.

Red mangrove (*Rhizophora mangle*) are perhaps the most charismatic of Florida's species. They ride the coastlines, perched on the edge of the edge—on the seaward side of coastal swamps and marshes, where the land fades imperceptibly into the salty depths. When wet, their bark takes on a reddish hue.

Nicknamed "the walking tree," the red mangrove's most distinctive feature is its spindly, interlocking root system. These stilt-like supports—known as prop roots—hold the main trunk of the tree above the high tide line. These prop roots also feature specialized pores called lenticels, which aid in the tree's respiration.

Braced at half a dozen angles in the soft mud below, the red mangrove is the wedding of two worlds—leafy green branches serve as an important rookery for seabirds such as the brown pelican. In the phalanx of their cantilevered prop roots, the red mangrove shelters an expansive nursery for Florida's most beloved fish, as well as a whole microscopic ecosystem of bacteria, algae, and fungi.

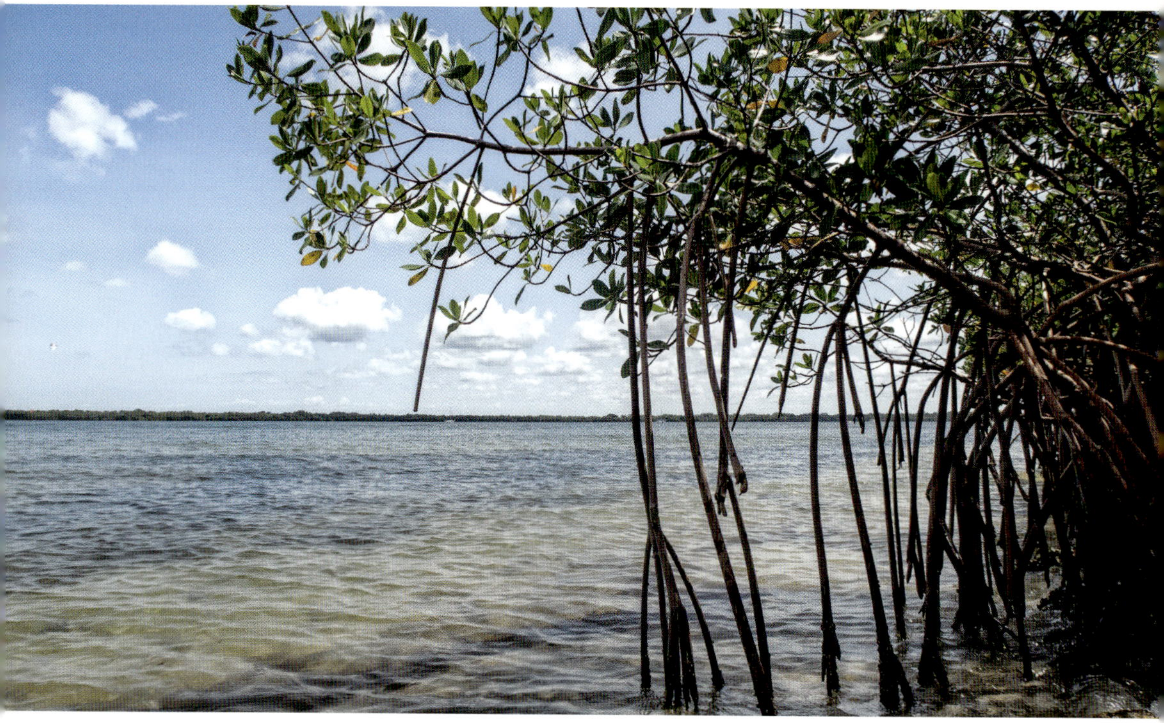

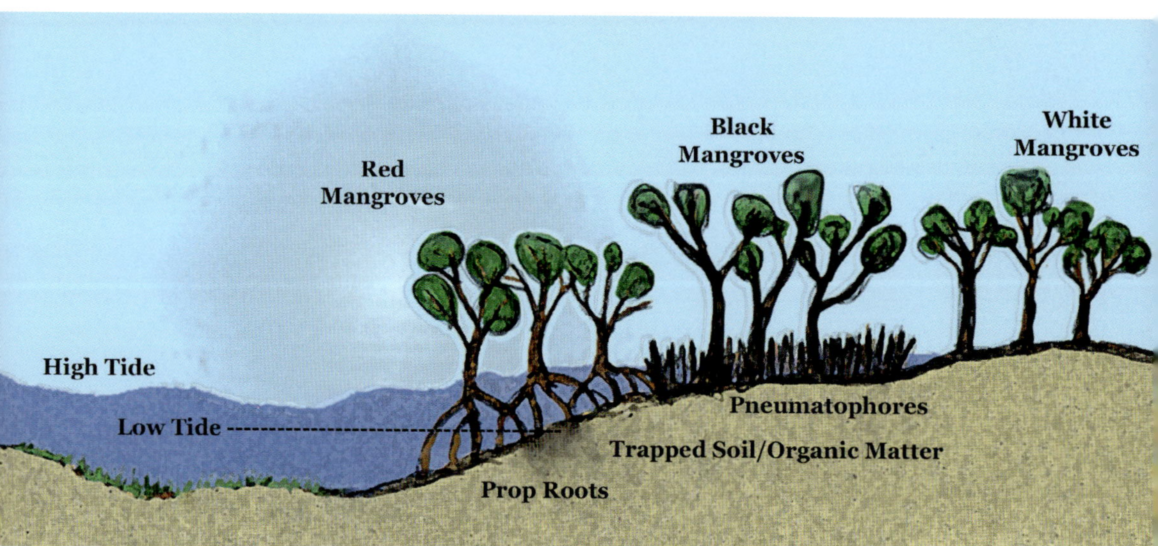

A simplified diagram of mangrove zonation.

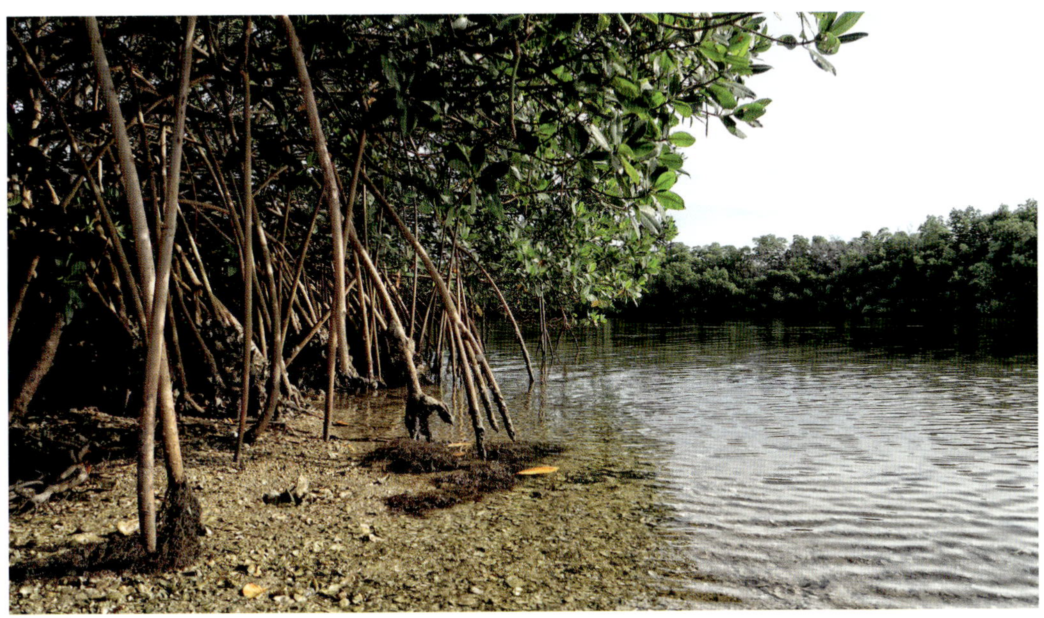

The distinctive crimson-tinted prop roots of the red mangrove stabilize the tree. Sometimes mangroves colonize a well-established oyster bed, as seen here, but just as often, the opposite is true—oysters anchor to the prop roots, filter feeding on the seawater that rises and falls with the tide.

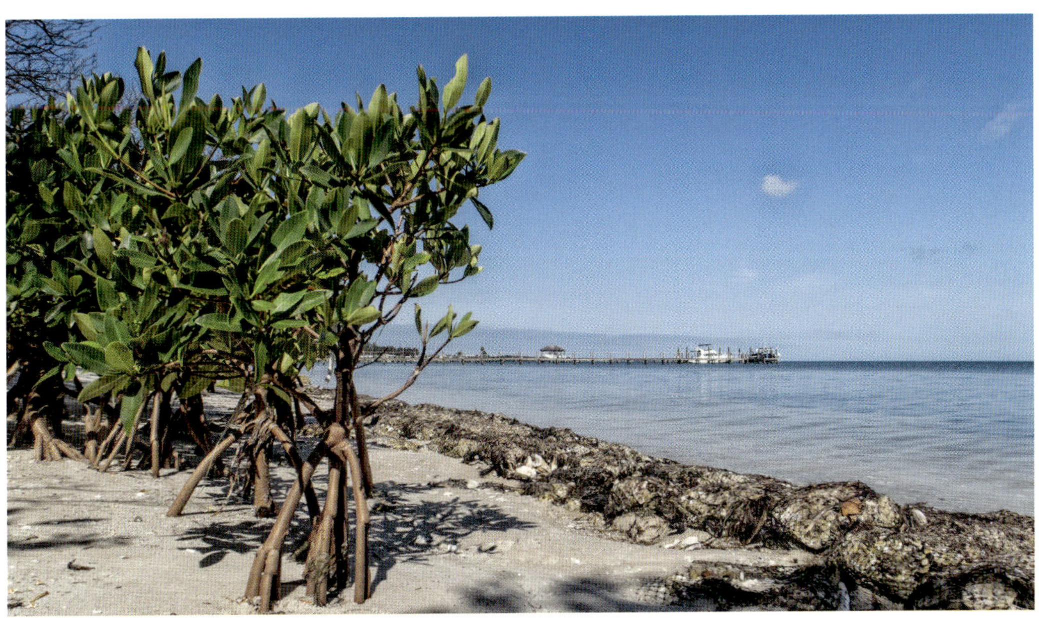

These oyster bags have been placed between juvenile red mangroves and the water's edge—a deliberate attempt to restore mangroves in an area that had previously been maintained as a beach. The prop roots of these mangroves will gradually knit together, forming a dense cover that renders the human-prepared bags redundant.

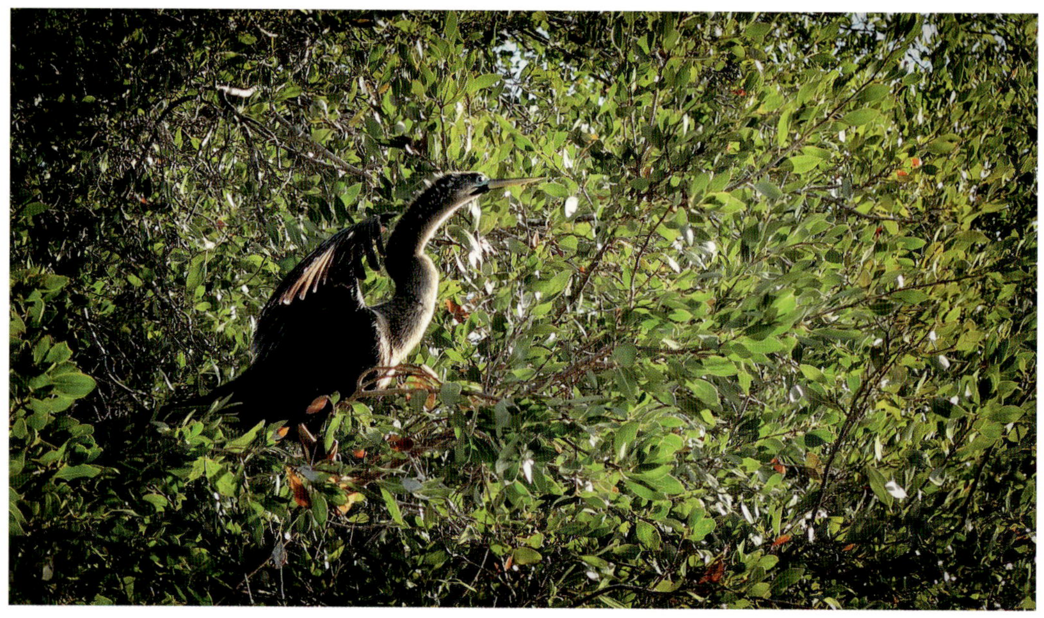

An anhinga dries its wings in the upper story of a red mangrove. This diving bird—along with its blue-eyed cousin the cormorant—are among the many species of birds who fish the brackish waters around a healthy mangrove forest.

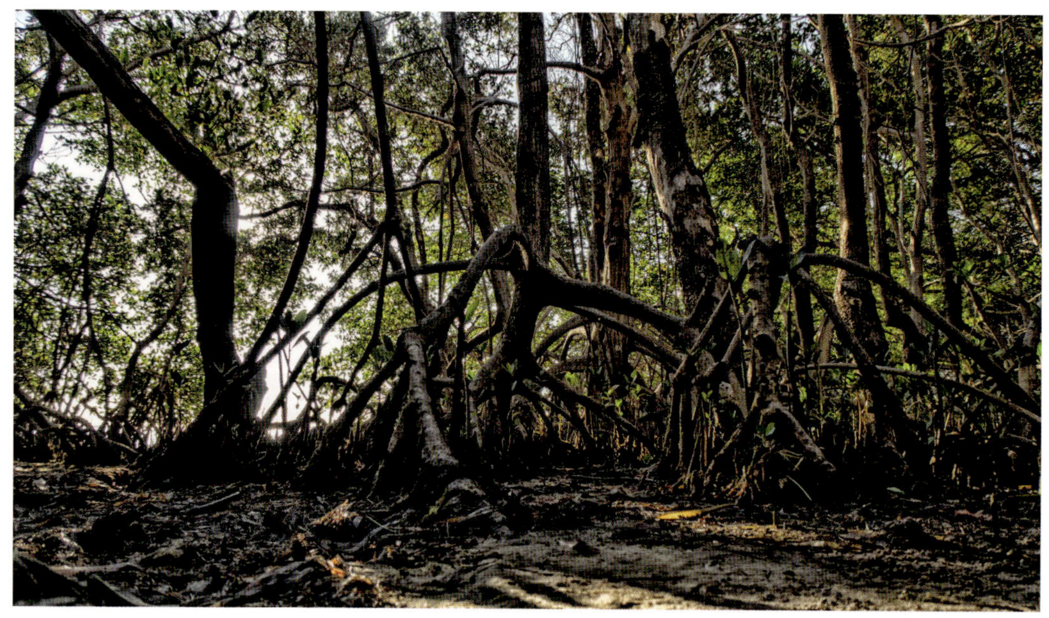

Gnarly-kneed red mangrove prop roots seem to clutch the forest floor with a level of determination that is almost visceral. Indeed, that soil is not going anywhere, and neither are the trees above—mangrove forests are incredibly resistant to erosion, stabilizing shorelines wherever they are found.

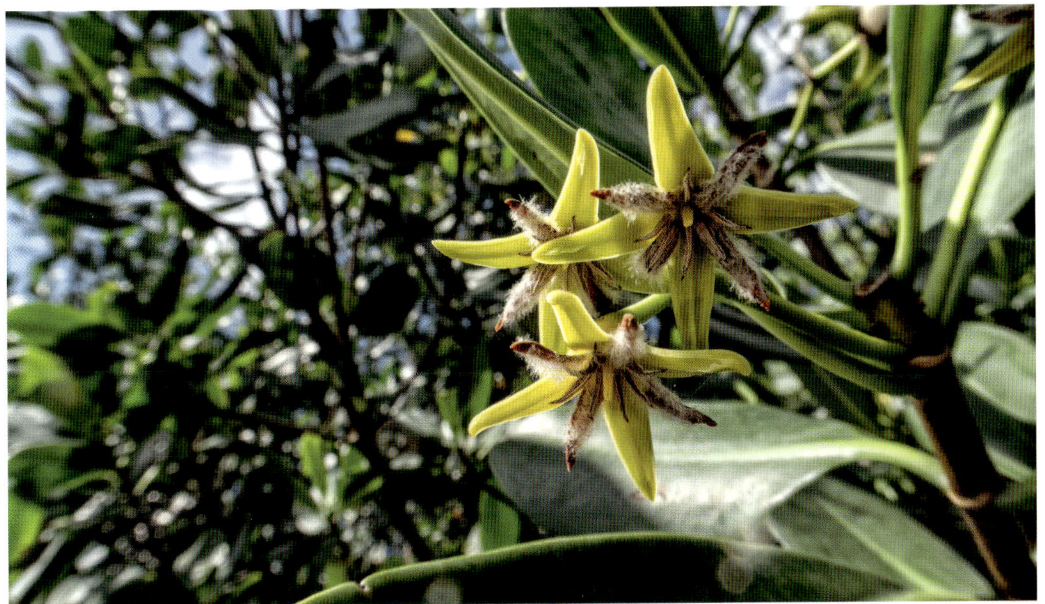

The banana yellow blossoms of a red mangrove. Flowers may appear year round, but are most common in spring and early summer.

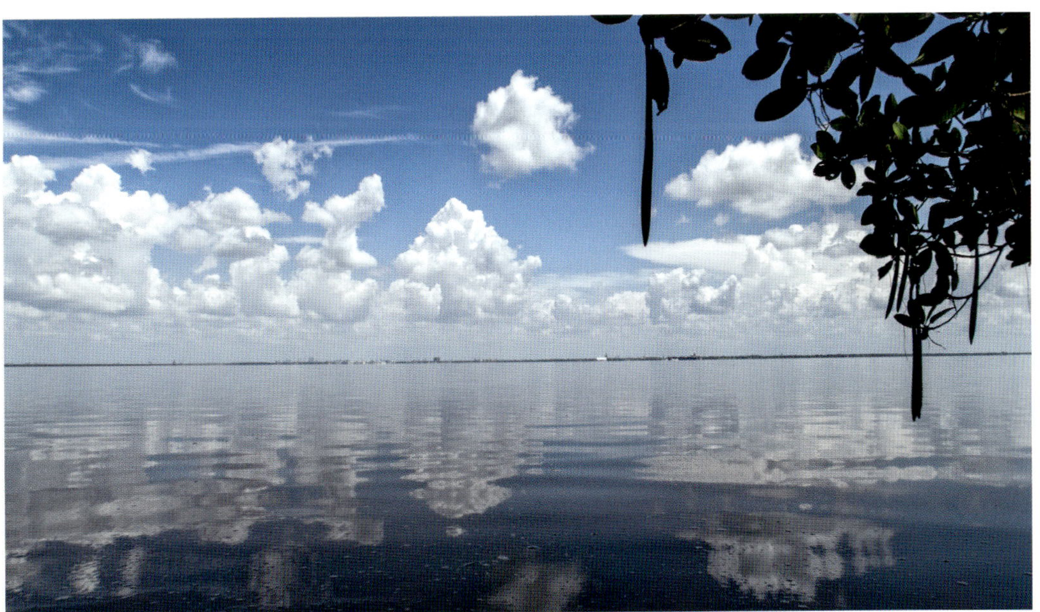

Those flowers will ultimately mature into a buoyant propagule shaped like a giant green bean—somewhere between 6 and 12 inches in length. After drifting on the surface of the water, sometimes for days, weeks, or months, a lucky propagule can take root on the shallow floor of an estuary, on a partially-submerged oyster bed, or anywhere that wave action is sufficiently gentle to bring the new plant to rest.

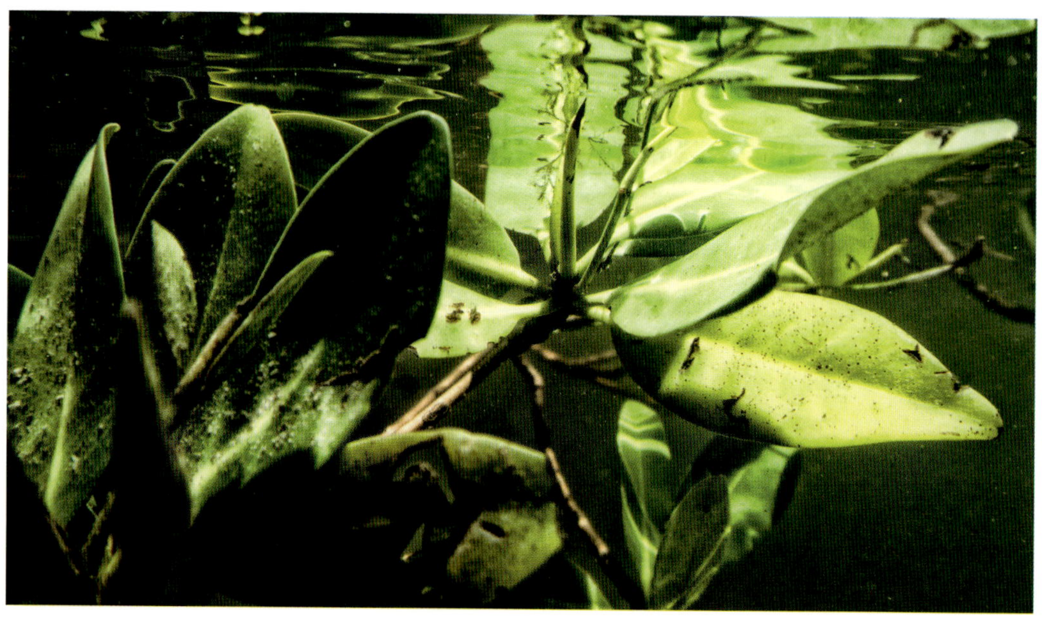

The lowest branch of a red mangrove tree, submerged at high tide.

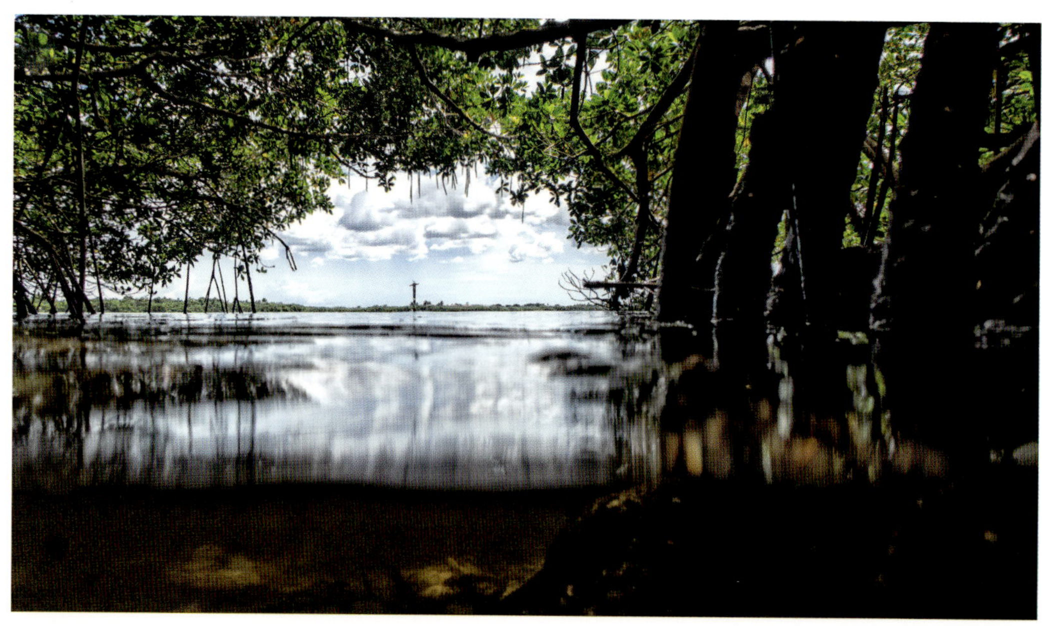

The prop roots of the red mangrove are so effective at trapping debris, that, given enough time, they can actually form new islands, raise the elevation of existing ones, and expand shorelines. If restored to their historic ranges, they could be an effective ally in humanity's urgent quest to halt the worst effects of climate change.

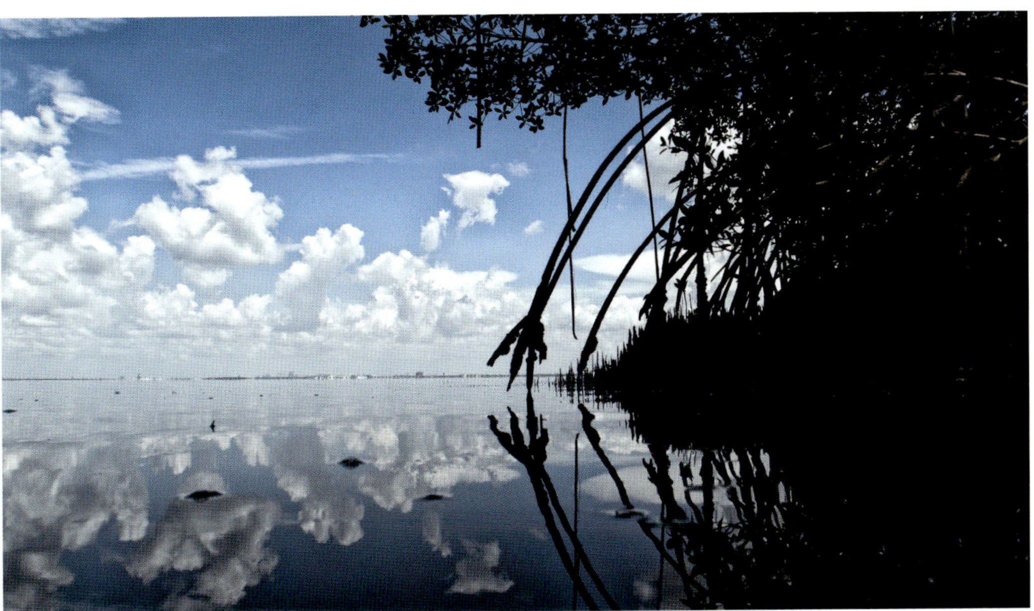

We all need somebody to lean on.

The range of the black mangrove (*Avicennia germinans*) often overlaps with that of the red mangrove. The black mangrove is most readily distinguished by its pneumatophores, which resemble woody, golem-like fingers grasping forth vertically from the earth. Similar to the prop roots of the red mangrove, pneumatophores are covered in lenticels—tiny pores that help to aerate the tree's roots. These "snorkels" allow the tree to thrive in saturated, anaerobic soil—facilitating the free exchange of carbon dioxide and oxygen, even when the tree's roots are otherwise inundated by saltwater.

Also like the prop roots of the red mangrove, these pneumatophores play an important role in stabilizing and even building up shorelines through the accumulation of soil and debris. A single well-developed tree may have as many as 1,000 pneumatophores, clutching the earth lest any precious grain of sand escape its anchorage.

Of Florida's three mangrove species, the white mangrove (*Laguncularia racemose*) grows farthest inland, generally above the high tide line—though it is perfectly capable of withstanding surge events and king tides. Unlike its black and red neighbors, its root system is not immediately distinguishable from other terrestrial trees. Its namesake white bark is covered in lenticels, which aid in respiration, similar to the ones that appear on the prop roots of the red mangrove. Its antenna-like clusters of greenish flowers look like alien pods cribbed from some sci-fi writer's farthest-fetched fantasy.

The white mangrove is most easily recognized by its leathery, elliptically-shaped leaves. These feature a small indentation instead of the pointed tip seen in nearby black and red mangrove leaves. White mangroves also have two distinctive bolt-like notches—known as nectaries—at the base of each leaf. These nectaries secrete sugars on which ants love to feed. In turn, the ants help to protect the white mangrove from other herbivorous insects who might dine on its leaves.

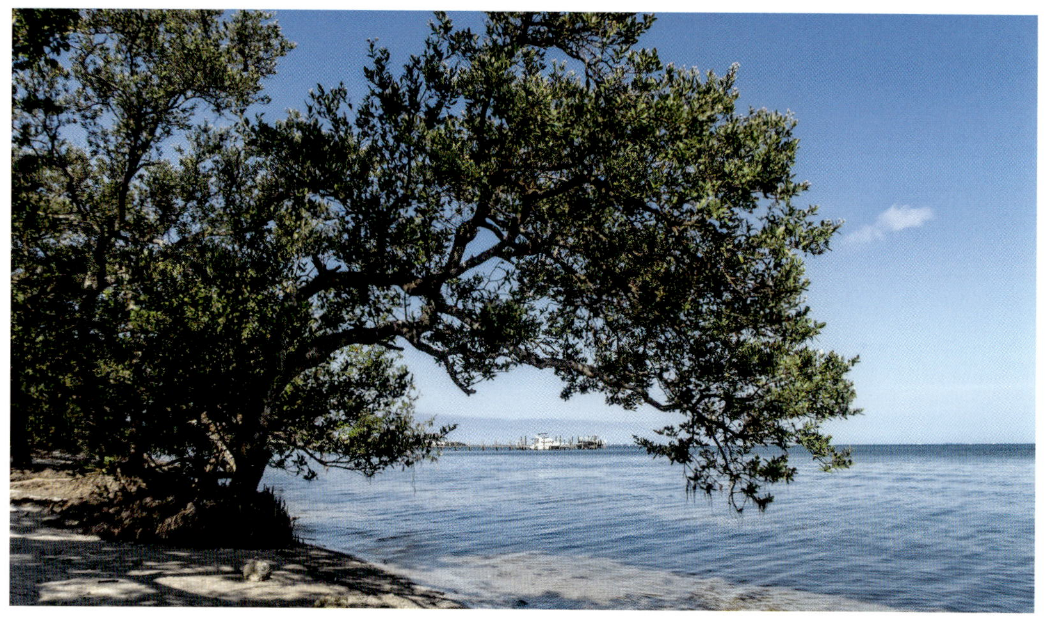

A black mangrove stakes out the high tide line.

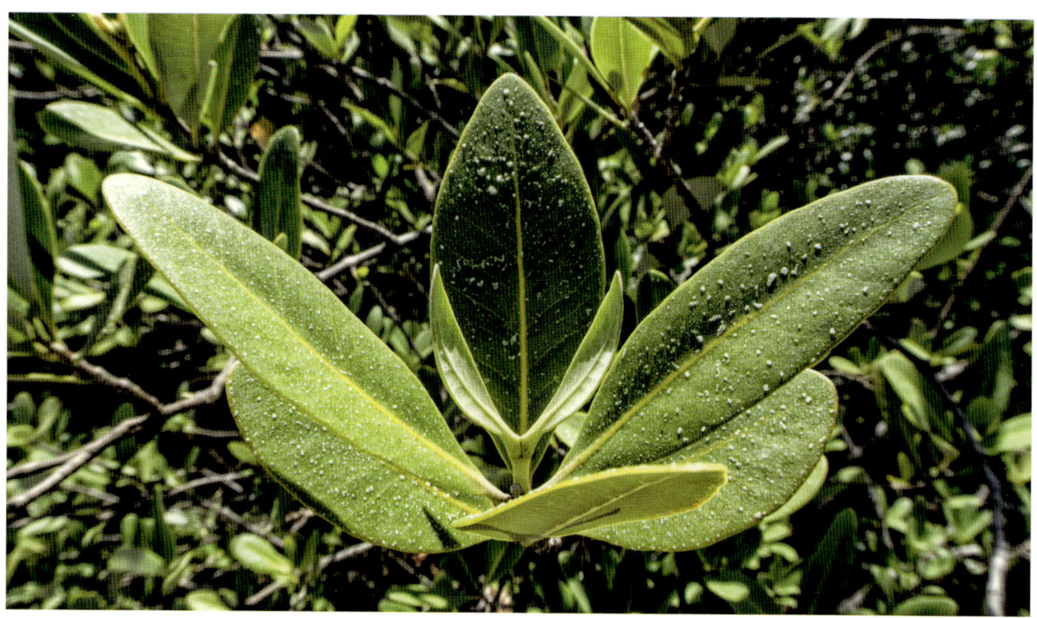

Excess salt is excreted through special glands in the leaves of the black mangrove, producing a delicate crystalline glaze that is completely harmless to the plant.

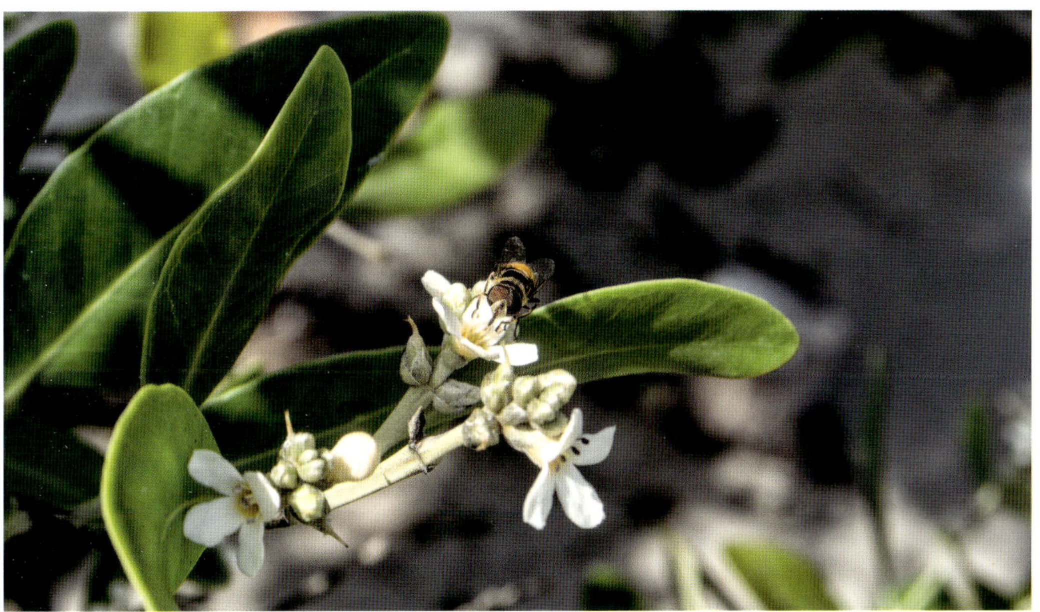

The black mangrove produces dainty white flowers in spring and summer. When pollinated, these will grow into a lima bean-shaped propagule. Unlike the propagules of the red mangrove, which can take root in the intertidal zone, the propagule of the black mangrove does best at the very edge of the high tide line.

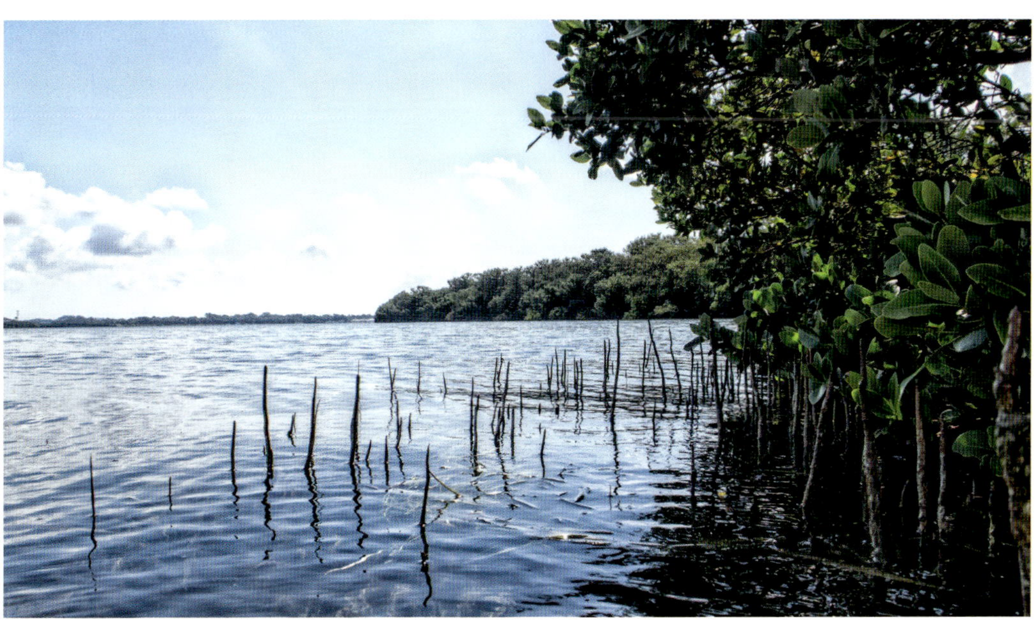

Black mangroves are most recognizable by their finger-like pneumatophores—their "air-breathing roots." These roots act like a snorkel, aiding in the tree's respiration even at high tide or in anaerobic soils that are hostile to most other plant life.

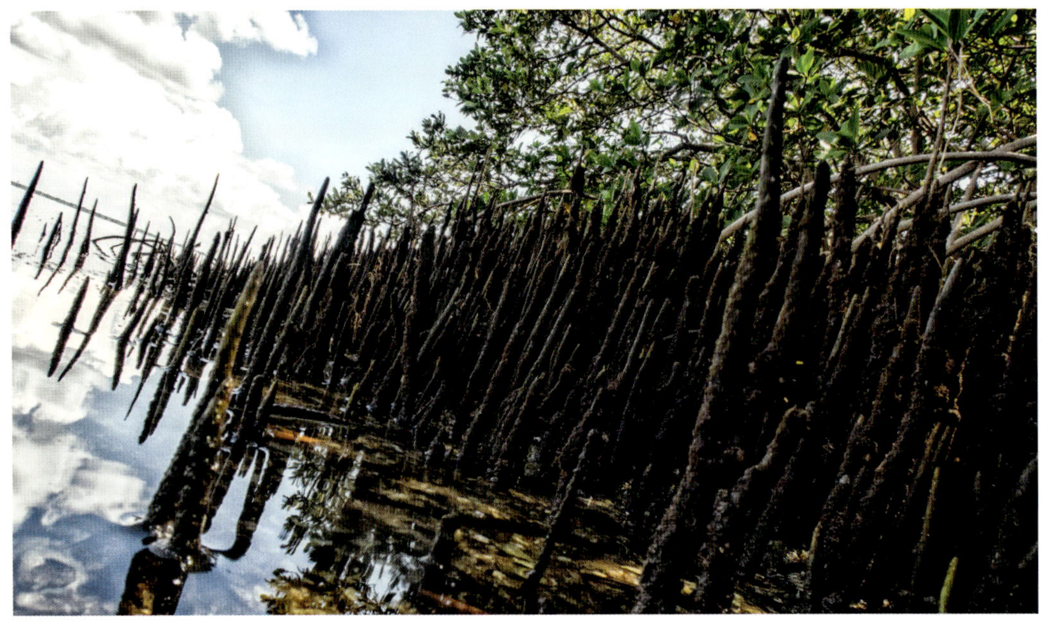

While the prop roots of the red mangrove are as rigid as a strong tree branch, the pneumatophore of the black mangrove is generally softer and more flexible—and thus, more easily damaged by clumsy humans. Give them plenty of space!

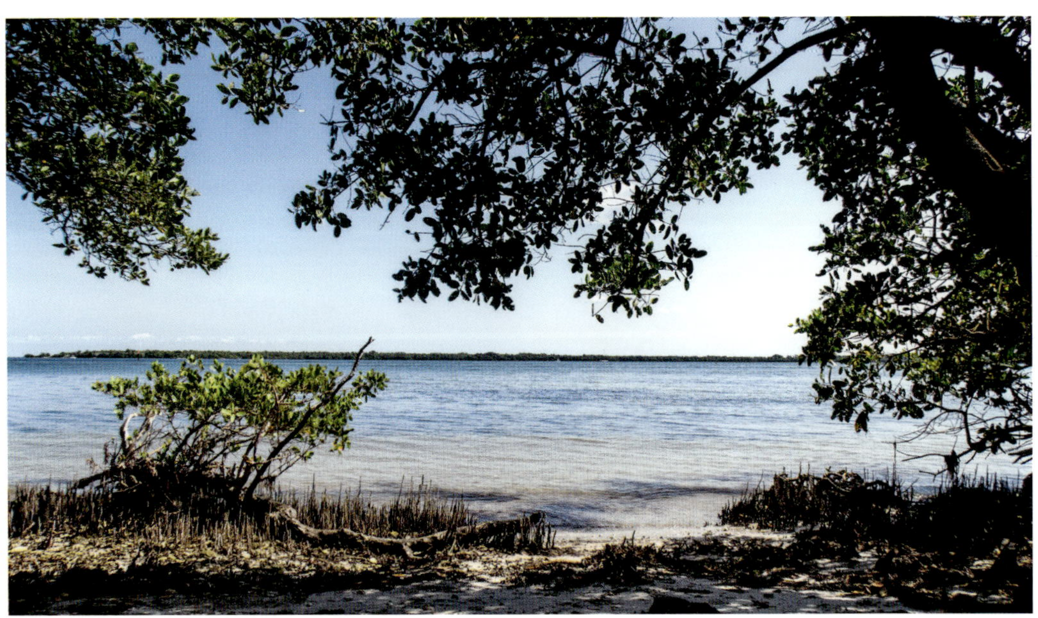

They might be giants—a well-established black mangrove provides shade and stability as a sapling, perhaps its own progeny, takes root.

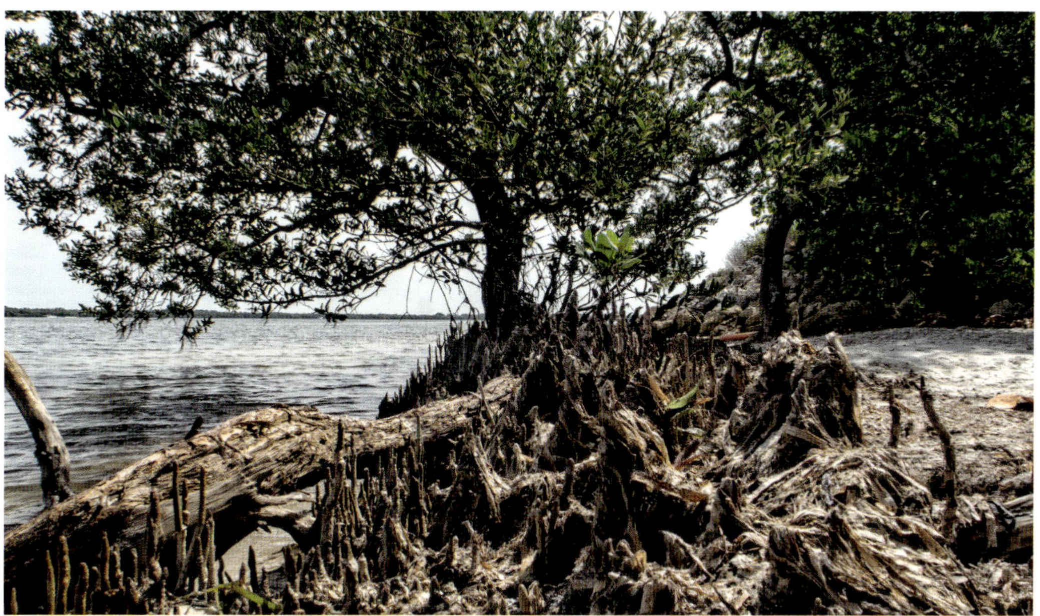

A bed of pneumatophores, like a bed of nails, has a way of ensnaring anything carried into its maw on the surf—in this case, seagrass, oysters broken from their anchorage, bits of driftwood, and plenty of particulate that is too small to immediately notice. It is a striking illustration of just how effectively these trees work with their red cousins to shore up their coastal habitat.

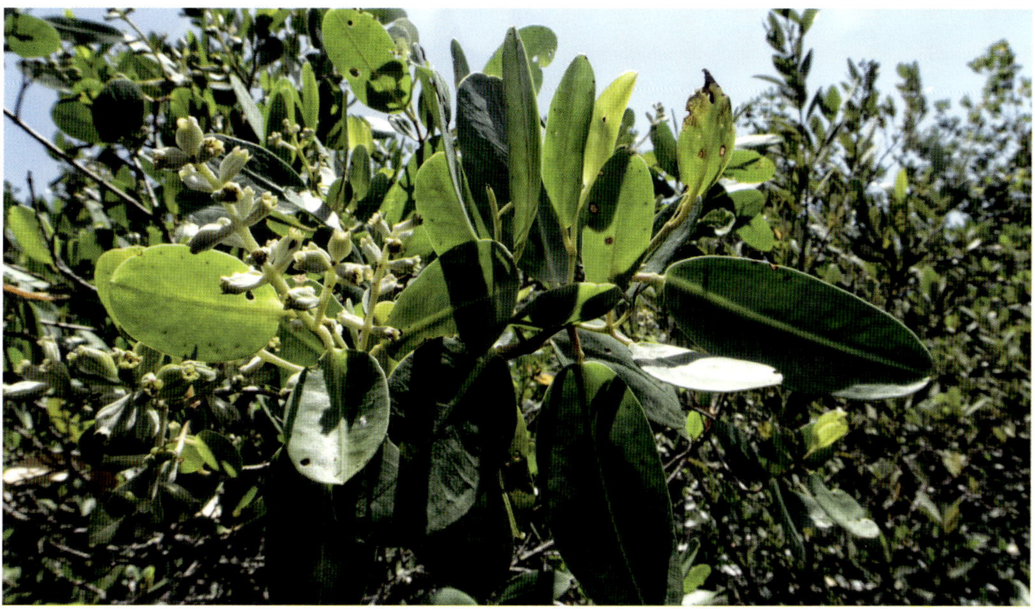

At first glance, the oblong leaves of the white mangrove might easily be mistaken for those of the red mangrove. More easily distinguishable are its elongated clusters of small white flowers, seen in the spring and early summer. In late summer, these ultimately turn into strands of pod-like propagules—a readily identifiable clue that you are looking at a white mangrove tree.

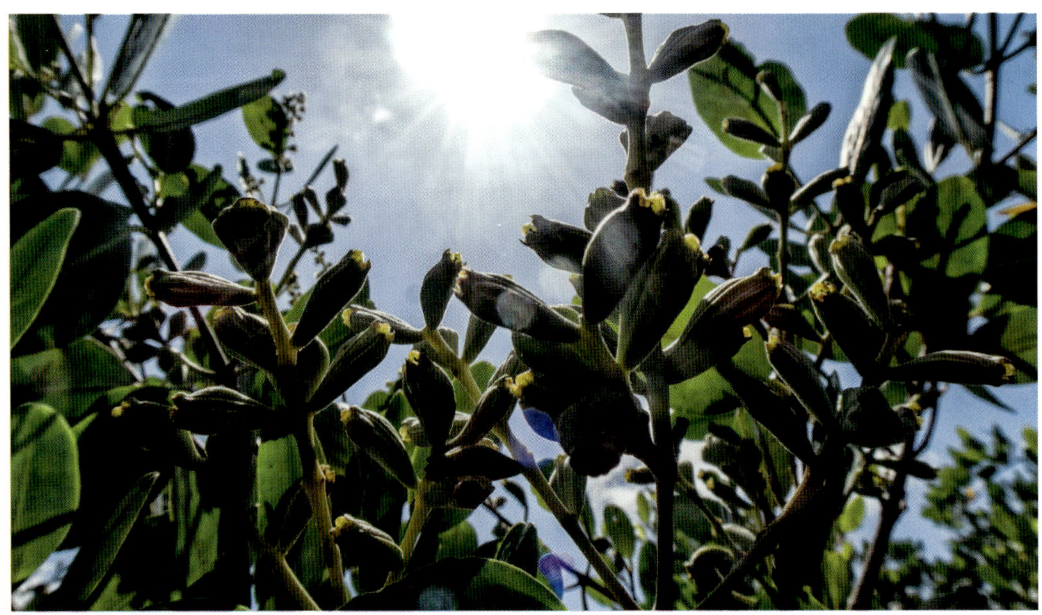

Unlike the propagules of the red and black mangrove, which begin to germinate while still attached to the parent tree, white mangrove propagules do so upon dispersal. While the propagules of the former two varieties are viable for between four months and a year, the white propagule is the least hardy of Florida's three mangrove species—it must take root above the high tide line within its first month.

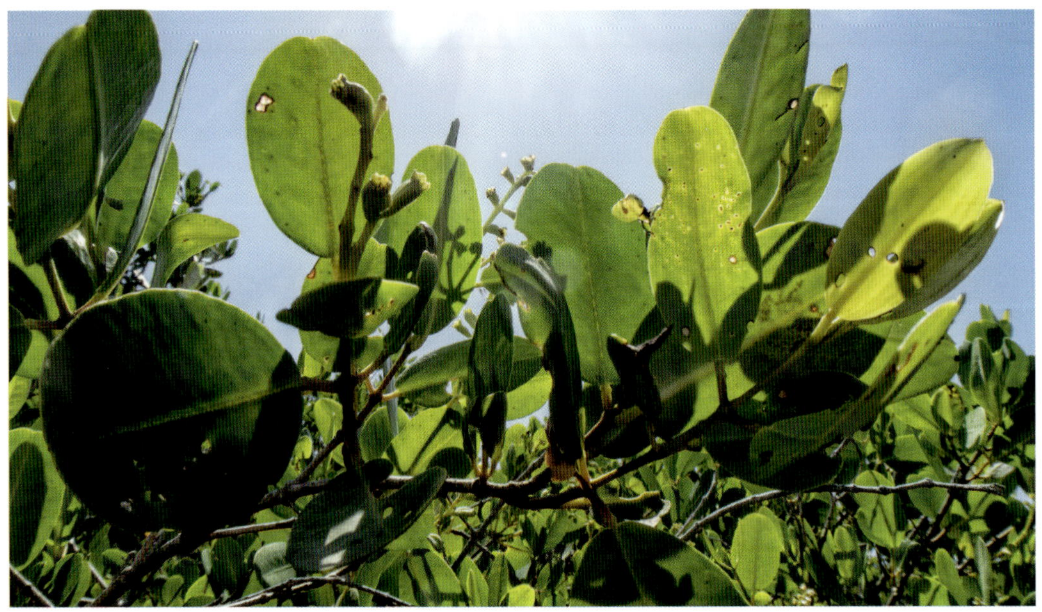

In contrast to their spider-like red neighbors and grasping black peers, the trunk and roots of a white mangrove look much like any other terrestrial tree. Indeed, of the three, the white mangrove grows farthest from shore. Its base is typically only submerged during flooding, surge events, or king tides.

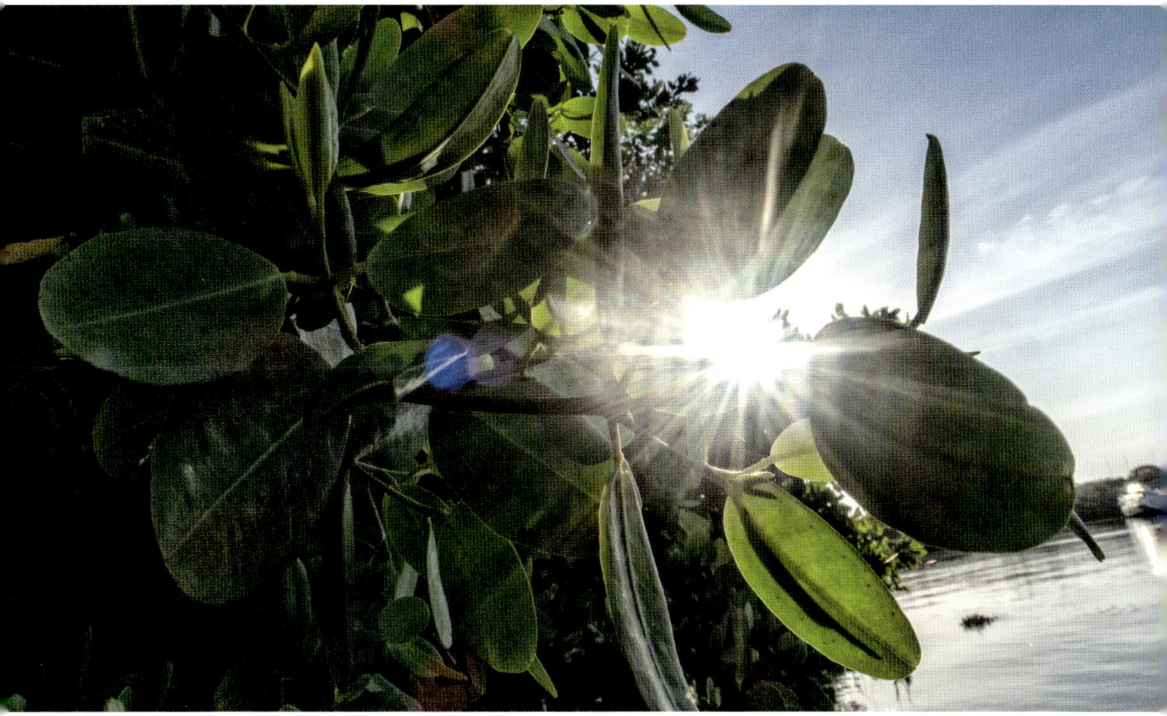

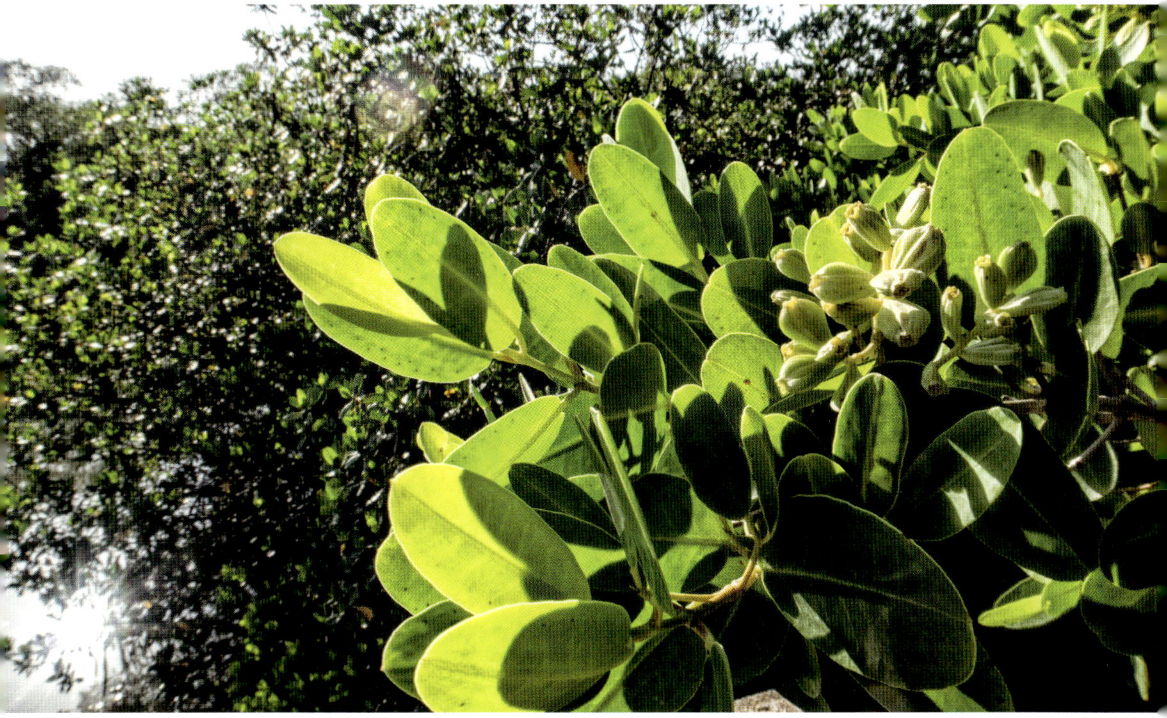

The red mangrove is an expert salt-excluder, meaning that it has the ability to exclude most sea salt right at the roots, even before it enters the tree's vascular system, leaving behind most salt molecules while slurping up the precious freshwater that the tree needs to live. Think of a straw stuck into a glass of soda that is chock-full of ice cubes—you are going to get a cool, refreshing drink, without any crunch of ice on your teeth.

While black and white mangroves are capable of limited salt exclusion at the roots, these species generally take a different tact against their saline surroundings. Both trees excrete excess salts in a kind of sweat from glands in their leaves. By late morning, the sweat has dried, leaving behind an enchanting crystalline glaze—the nearest these trees will ever come to the kiss of a wintery frost.

The red mangrove is not an efficient excreter, perhaps explaining why it is actually the least salt-tolerant of the three varieties. Salt accumulates in its leaves, which, one by one, turn yellow and drop off to the forest floor below. It is tempting to view these leaves as performing some sort of sacrificial function, but research suggests that the yellow leaves are not accumulating salt at a notably higher rate than the leaves around them; rather, they have simply reached the threshold of their tolerance and drop away so that a fresh green leaf can begin the cycle anew.

It is a sure sign of our own species' chronic narcissism that any conversation about nature ultimately comes around to the question, "But what does X do for humans?"

The mangrove can hold its own on this self-centered line of inquiry, so let us get right to it.

The three species of mangrove often grow together, woven into a spectacularly productive ecosystem known as a mangrove forest. Such a forest is capable of absorbing

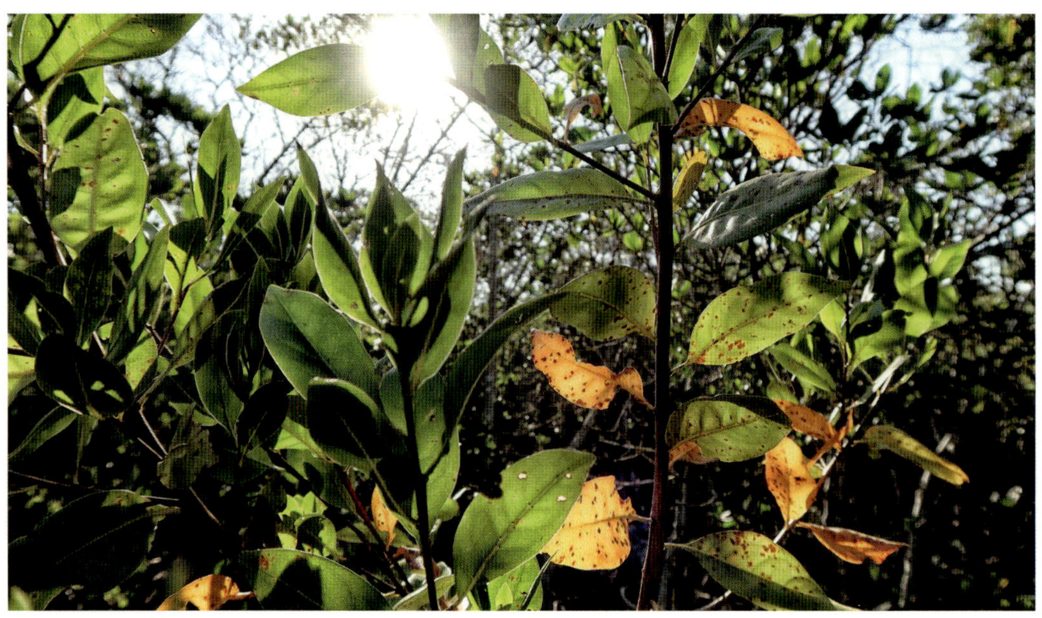

These gorgeous golden leaves interspersed among vivid green are the sign of a healthy red mangrove. Salt accumulation in these leaves causes the color change. They will eventually drop to the forest floor—leaving the rest of the tree to thrive with that much less salt in its system.

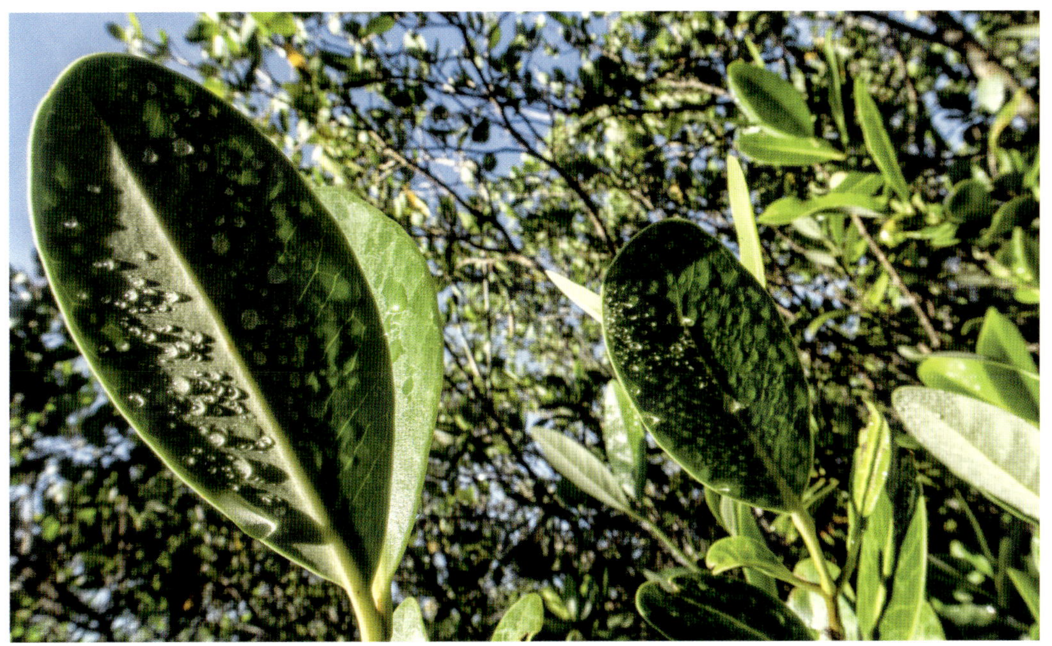

This is not mere condensation—soon, the water on this black mangrove will evaporate, leaving behind a harmless salty residue on the leaf's surface. White mangroves excrete salt in a similar fashion.

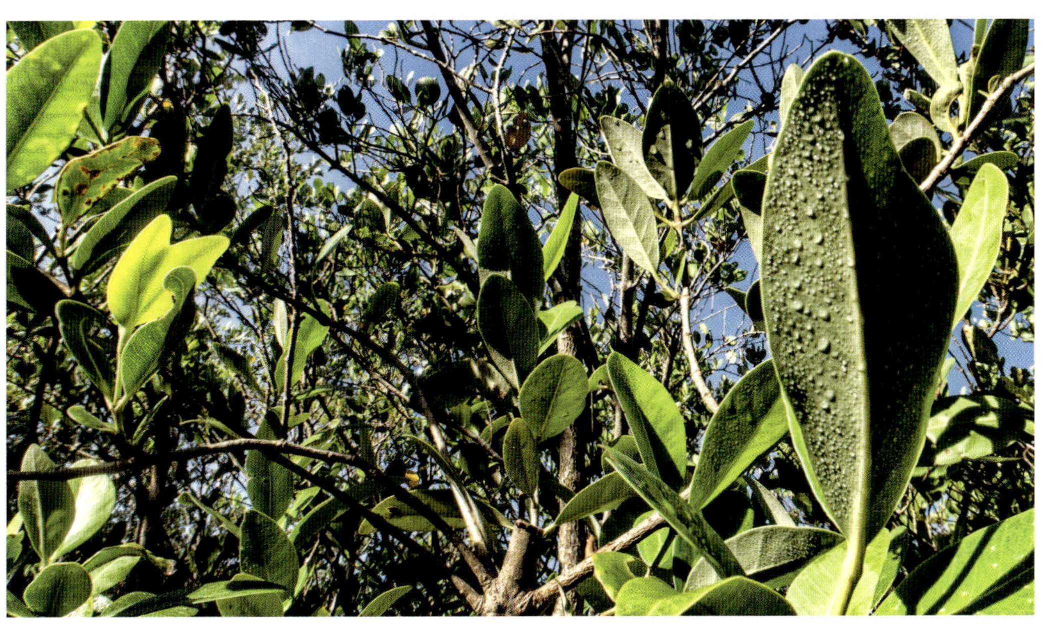

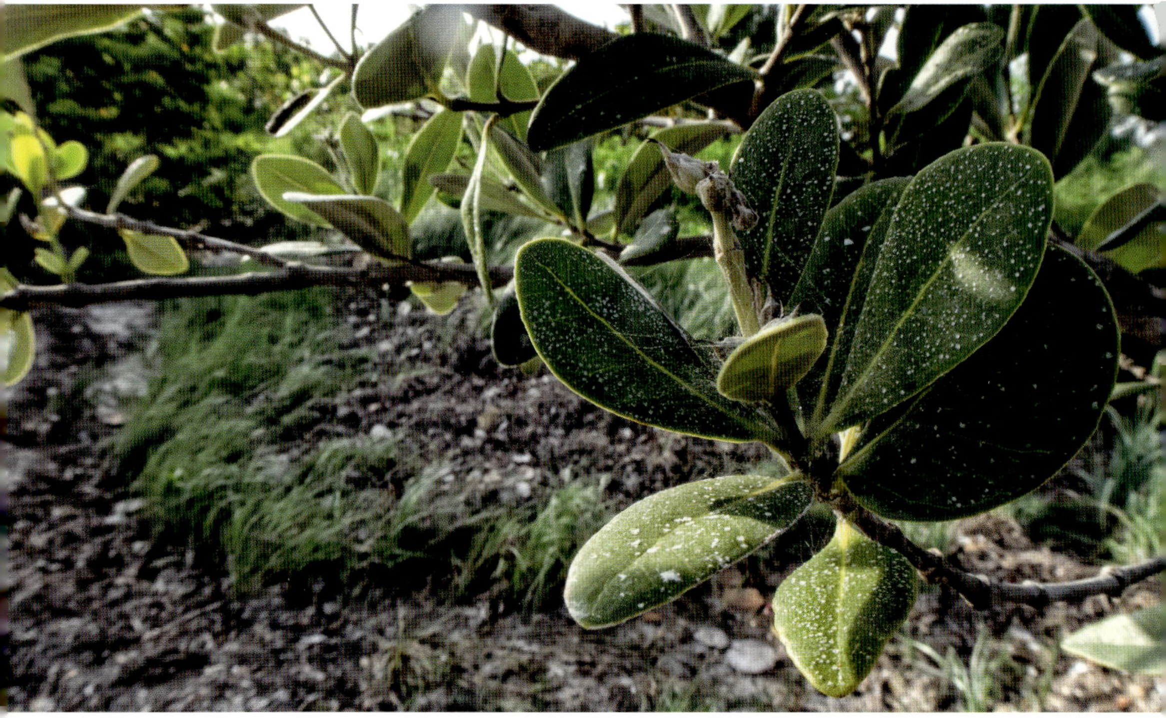

Salt crystals glistening on the leaves of a black mangrove.

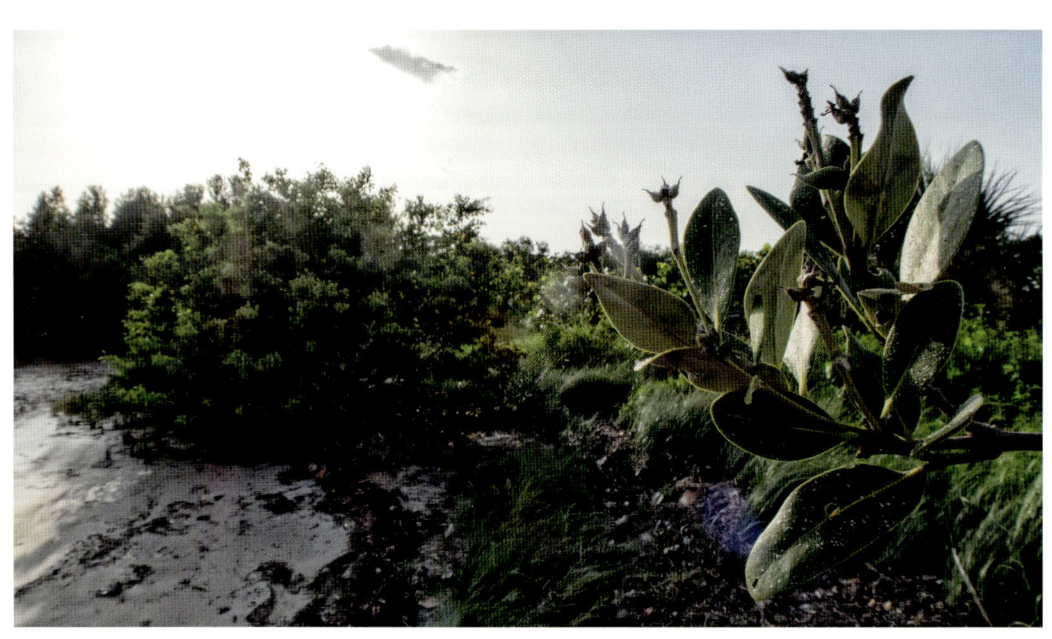

up to 76 percent of storm surge during a hurricane, of trapping debris and detritus brought in and out by the tides, and of retaining a great deal of soil that would otherwise erode and be swept out to sea.[1] As such, mangrove forests provide a vital natural barrier against the violence of hurricanes, as well as the day-to-day wear and tear caused by tides, currents, and waves—shielding both human infrastructure, as well as other less salt- and flood-resistant inland biomes.

For this reason, mangrove forests are sometimes referred to by urban planners and ecologists as "green infrastructure"—an evocative term that emphasizes the potential for these natural ecosystems to create more resilient, livable communities nearby. According to The Nature Conservancy, Florida's coastal mangroves prevented around $1.5 billion in flood damages during 2017's Hurricane Irma, in the process sparing half a million people from the worst of the storm. By most estimates, a healthy mangrove forest is a far cheaper—and more effective—solution to hurricane mitigation than levees, seawalls, riprap, or, really, any other method of engineered "grey infrastructure" devised by humans.

One study, conducted at Merritt Island National Wildlife Refuge (MINWR) near NASA's Kennedy Space Center, found that a 2-meter-wide strip of mangroves can reduce the height of waves by as much as 90 percent.[2] The same study estimates that on an annual basis, coastal wetlands (including mangrove forests) provide around $23.5 billion in protection against major storm events in the U.S. alone. This result jives with other studies suggesting that during the 2004 Indian Ocean tsunami, communities shielded by mangroves fared better than those that sat behind artificial breaks.[3] What is more, mangroves not only reduce wave action, but wind speeds as well, creating a sort of "wind shadow" on the landward side of an incoming storm.

Show me the seawall that can do all of that—let alone for an effective net cost of free.

Mangroves have another advantage over simple manmade barriers—they are vital in maintaining biodiversity in neighboring ecosystems.

Mangrove tree detritus—as well as the waste of the many birds, crabs, snakes, lizards, and other creatures who call the upper portions of the trees home—provide the basis of a food web that supports a multitude of juvenile fish who live out the first stages of their lives hidden among the vast thickets of red mangrove prop roots. Tiny spotted seatrout (*Cynoscion nebulosus*), gray snapper (*Lutjanus griseus*), and red drum (*Sciaenops ocellatus*) are all protected from their gargantuan fishy elders—who might, in open waters, swallow a whole school of small fry in a single go.

Those open waters are cleaner for the presence of mangroves, too. The prop roots of the red mangrove form important anchors onto which a great variety of shellfish attach. These include oysters and barnacles—filter feeders who strain seawater for their sustenance. In the process, they moderate levels of pollutants, algae, and bacteria. Properly decomposed, the waste found on a mangrove forest floor is gradually flushed into surrounding ecosystems. With the ebb and flow of the tides, it provides vital nutrients for all manner of other small marine life.

Like so many Roombas, horseshoe crabs shuffle along the nutrient-dense margins of the mangrove forest, scavenging and fulfilling a similar clean-up niche on-the-go.

The mangrove forest, in other words, is perhaps the indispensable food web link in our estuaries and coastal waters. Lose the mangroves, and surrounding populations fall into a precipitous decline.

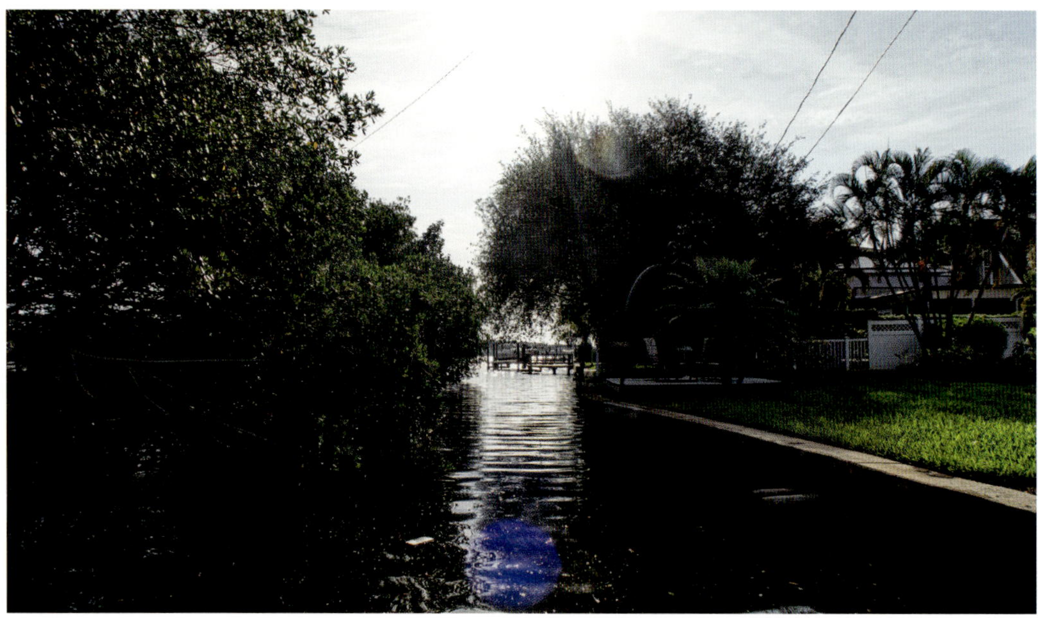

A cross-section of coastal Florida. A city park stands across a drainage canal from several private homes. Green infrastructure is often relegated to public property, as homeowners opt for expensive, yet comparatively ineffective grey infrastructure. Seawalls like this one might make for a better view of the water, but there is a definite tradeoff.

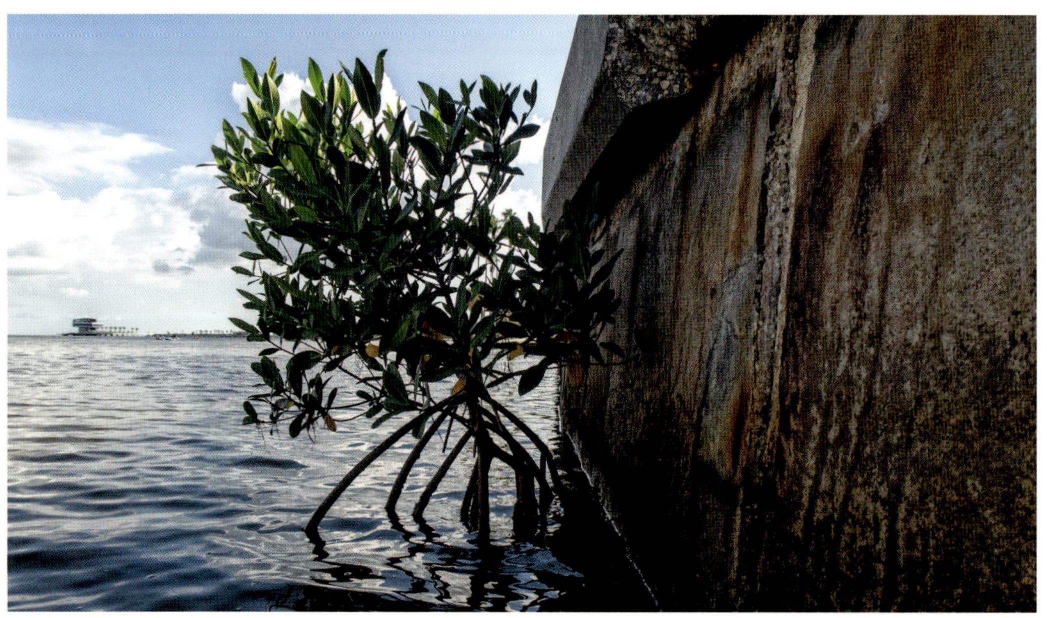

In contrast to a robust fringe of mangroves, a seawall does not absorb waves and surge—like echoes in a loud gymnasium, it scatters them, contributing to an environment that is overall more choppy, chaotic. What is more, a seawall does nothing whatsoever to protect the area behind it from wind.

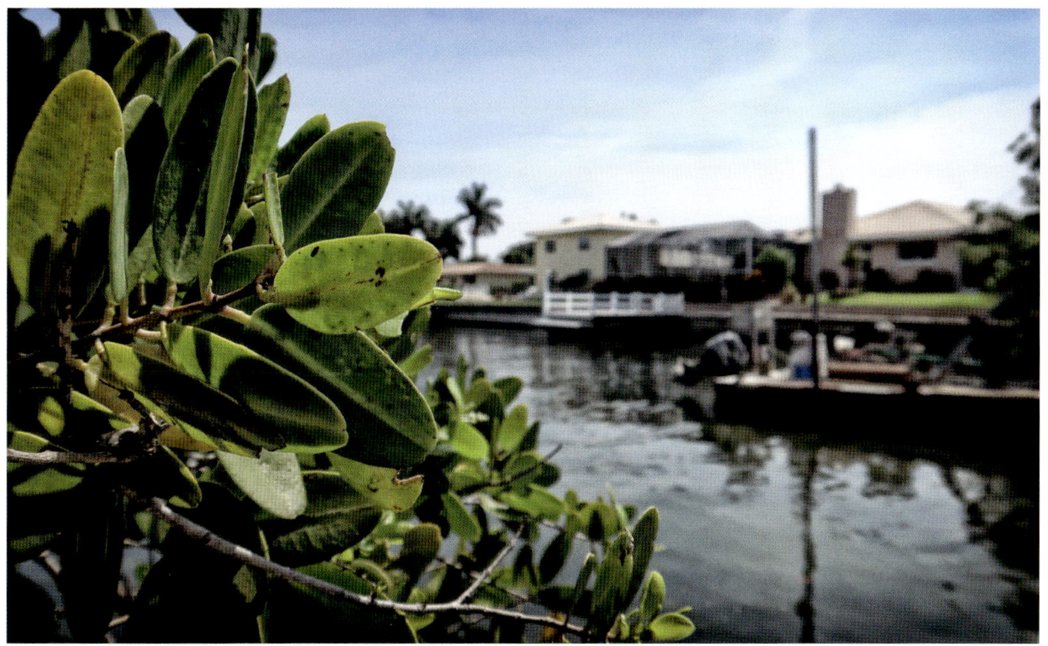

The riparian fringe—a liminal zone of mangroves on the edge of the water. Along Florida's increasingly developed coastline, these vestigial stands of trees—hemmed in by seawalls and regular trimming by homeowners and HOAs—can offer only token benefits to the ecosystems around them.

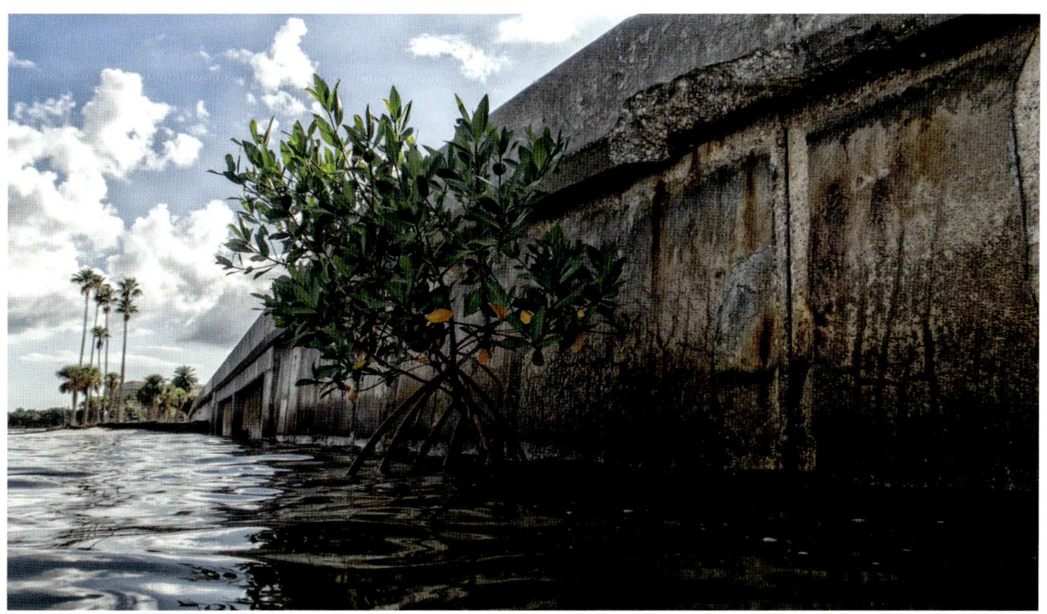

This red mangrove is a pioneer, gaining a foothold in front of a municipally-owned seawall on St. Petersburg's waterfront. Given time—and left to their own devices—red mangroves could likely colonize much of this shallow stretch of the Tampa Bay estuary, just as they would much of their former south Florida range.

Other fish supported by the web of life that extends into this liminal space include jack (*Caranx spp.*), sheepshead (*Archosargus probatocephalus*), and goliath grouper (*Epinephelus itajara*)—all favorites of Florida's fishermen.

According to the state's Department of Environmental Protection, Florida's seafood industry is worth somewhere in the ballpark of $7.6 billion and provides 109,000 jobs.[4] Something like 80 percent of the industry's catch is comprised of species that breed in mangrove forests or of species who feed primarily on those species. Florida's fishermen and the restaurants serving their catch are, in a very real sense, part of the extended mangrove ecosystem—and by all rights, should be some of the loudest opponents to the coastal development that continues to imperil this vulnerable ecosystem (more on that later in the book, though).

At least 175 distinct species of birds nest and feed in Florida's mangrove forests. Some birds, such as roseate spoonbills and brown pelicans breed almost exclusively in mangroves. Species such as osprey, bald eagles, egrets, and anhinga can live their whole lives fishing the productive waters in and around a healthy stand of mangroves.

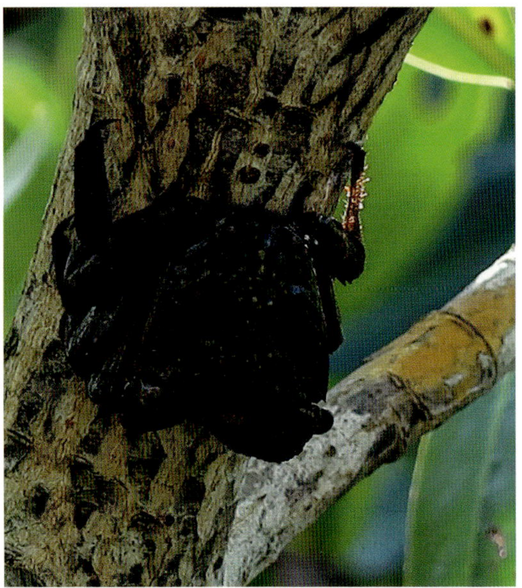
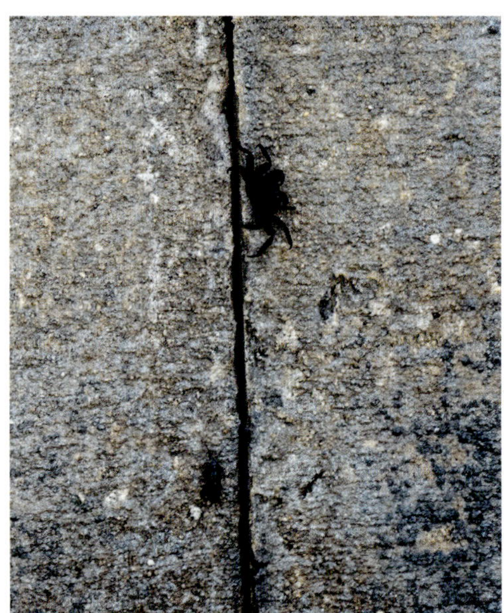

Above left: The mangrove tree crab is easy to miss—diminutive, stealthy, and shy, they also seem to creep right around to the far side of a branch at your approach. In reality, they are omnipresent, subsisting on a steady diet of red mangrove leaves, both living and dead, commuting with the tides between the muddy forest floor and the upper reaches of the canopy.

Above right: All along Florida's coastline, the destruction of mangroves means that this creature has had to adapt to life in the crevices of seawalls. Under these conditions, the mangrove tree crab becomes omnivorous—and the 200,000 juveniles produced by the average female in any given year are more vulnerable to predation, primarily by birds who take advantage of a relative lack of cover.

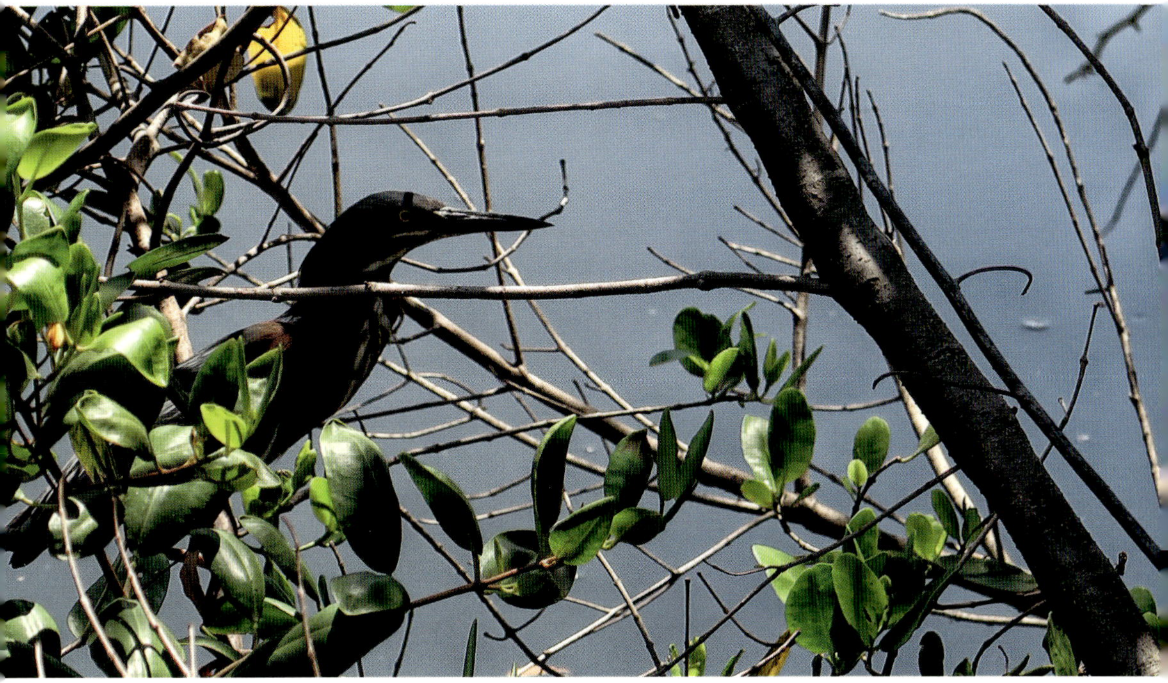

A green heron, one of the many varieties of shorebirds content to spend most of their lives in a healthy mangrove forest.

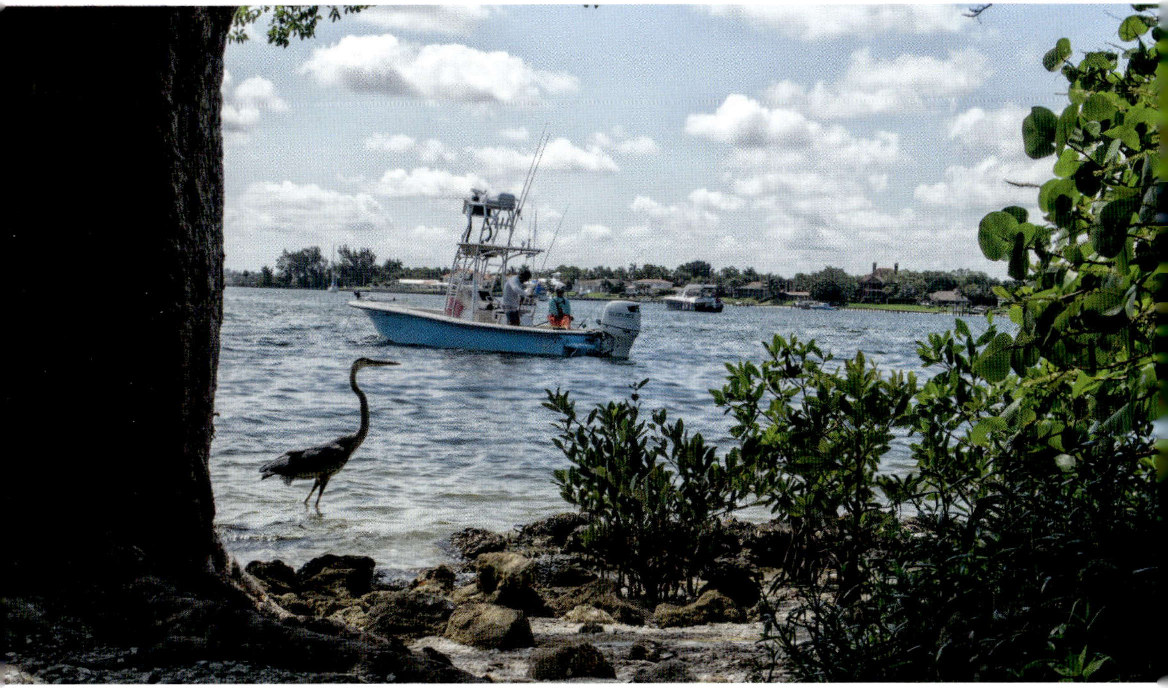

A great blue heron leading human fisherman to the catch.

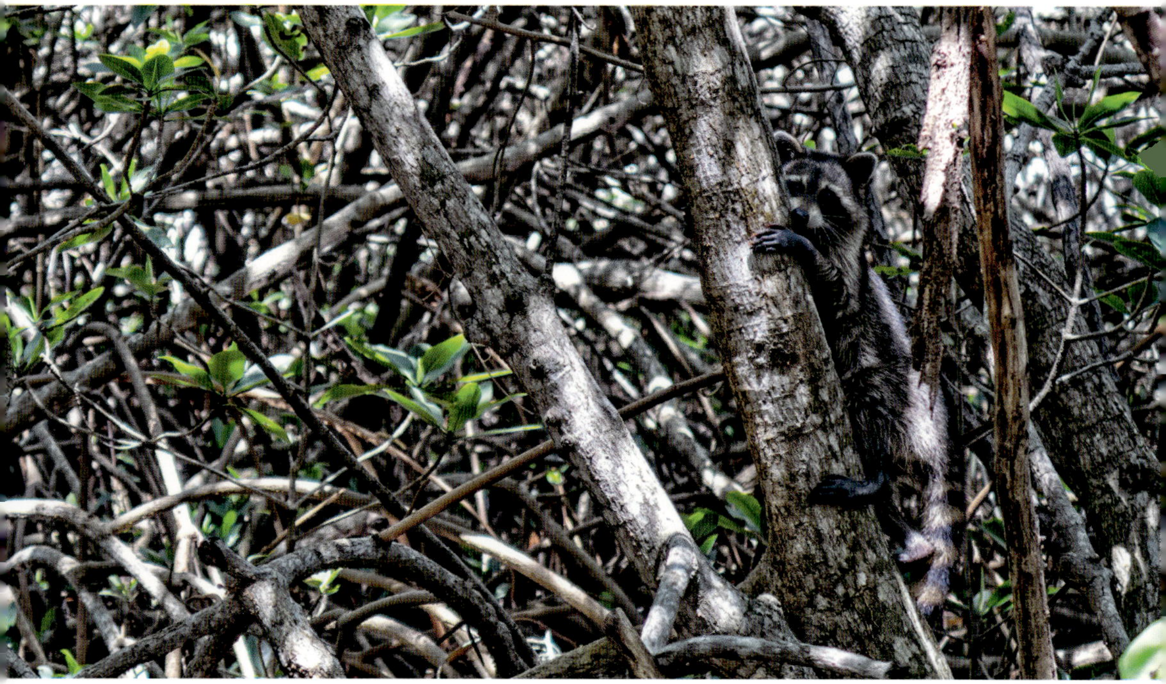

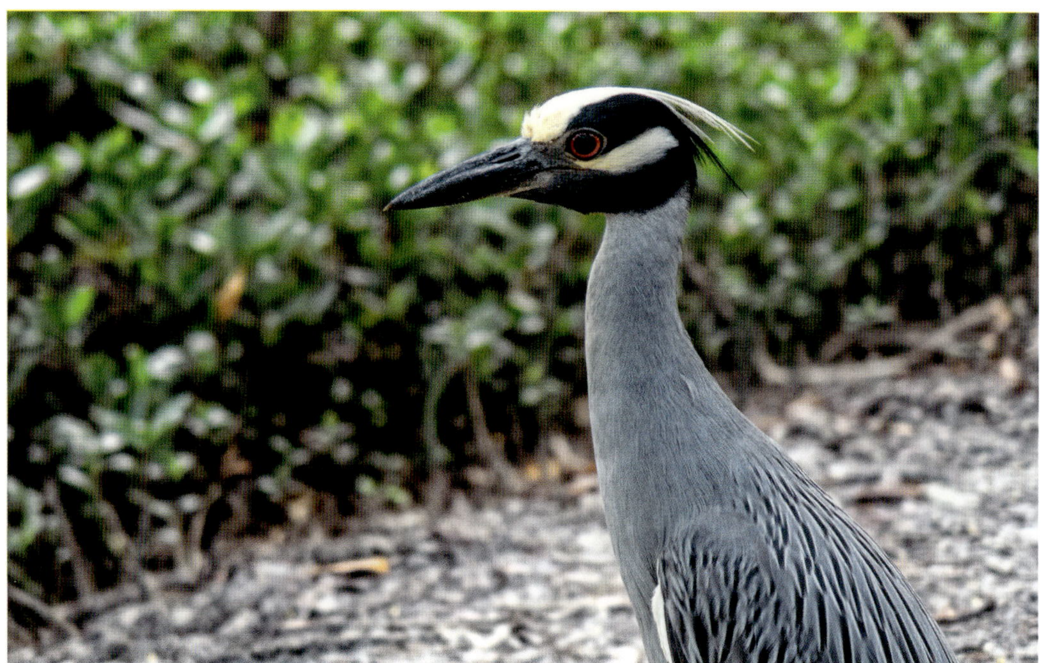

The highly adaptable raccoon is at home amidst the spindly legs of the red mangrove, feasting on the crabs, lizards, and fish that also live there.

A yellow-crowned night-heron on the forest's edge.

2

A CORNUCOPIA
IF YOU CAN KEEP IT

For around 12,000 years, likely since humans first entered the Florida peninsula, mankind has occupied a prominent niche within mangrove ecosystems. Through the wonders of archaeology, we know that the astounding productivity of Florida's mangroves was apparent to Florida's earliest peoples.

Middens are the refuse piles of the prehistoric world. These large heaps—filled with shells and bones from oysters, welch, jack, and other marine species whose life cycles wend their way through the prop roots of the red mangrove—reveal the hearty diet of Florida's coastal peoples. Based on this evidence, as well as on archaeology conducted elsewhere in their settlements and on the written accounts of Spanish explorers, there is little to suggest that these ancient societies farmed maize, beans, squash, or any other staple foods on any meaningful scale, if at all.

Rather, the food surplus of Florida's coastal civilizations—the Calusa, the Manasota, the Tocobaga, and so many others—is largely a testament to the prodigious nutritional abundance bursting forth from Florida's mangrove forests. The mangrove was a stand-in for the fertile river valleys, which gave rise to other complex civilizations elsewhere in the world, from the Yellow to the Nile.[1]

To say it again, mangroves were the cornerstone of civilization in ancient Florida.

Florida's indigenous coastal societies were neither primitive nor poor. Based on the intricacy of their pottery, architecture, and tools, as well as their vigorous participation in trade networks extending as far away as Cuba and the Great Lakes, we know that they achieved some meaningful division of labor within their society. These coastal peoples were not eking out a diminished existence at subsistence level. Undoubtedly, they worked for their bounty, but they were well-enough nourished to undertake massive construction projects—large ceremonial structures, canals, and dikes. Since south Florida offers little in the way of stone suitable for building or toolmaking, these clever peoples turned to the next best available material—the calcium-rich shells of conchs, bivalves, and other mollusks present in abundance in and around their coastal realm.

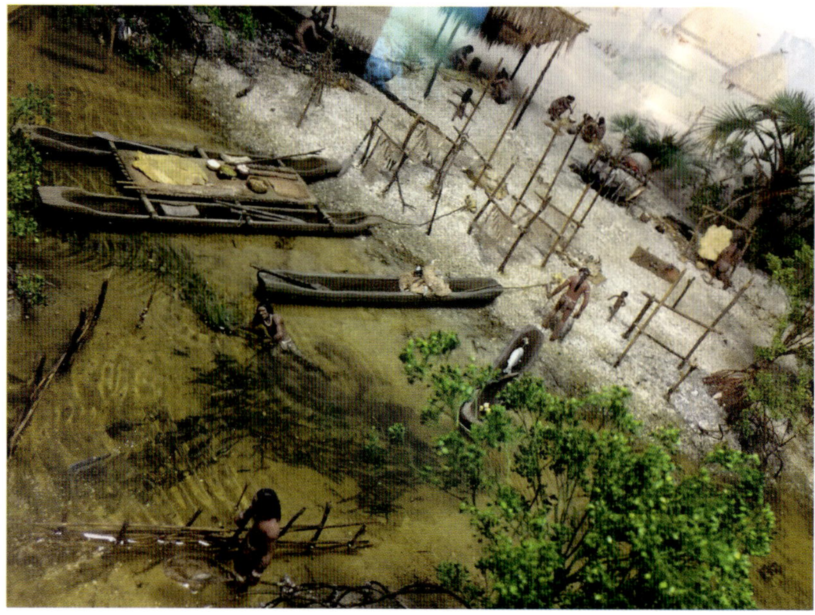

A diorama representing life in the mangroves as it must have been for any number of the native societies lining Florida's pre-contact coasts. These peoples lived in relative comfort and prosperity, largely on the bounty of the mangrove ecosystem around them. (*Florida Museum of Natural History*)

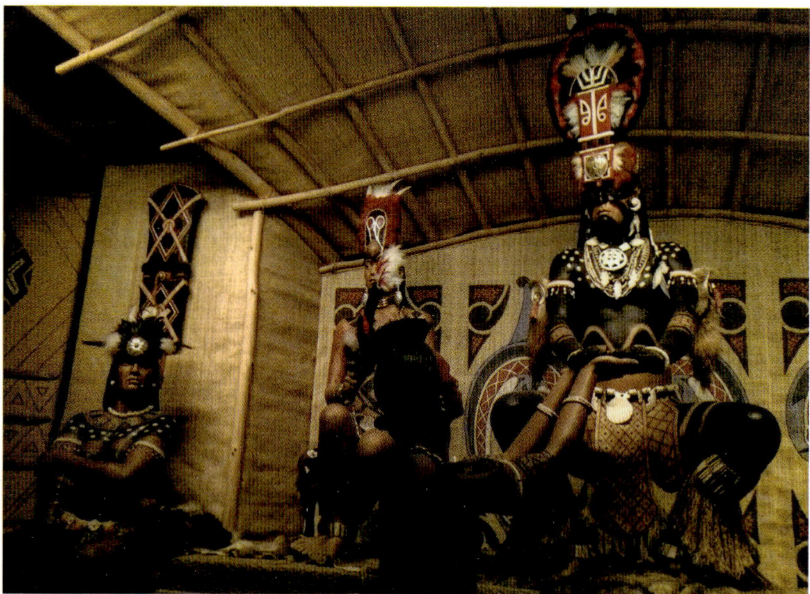

A depiction of the great Calusa chief—called Carlos by the Spanish. There exists little evidence to suggest that the Calusa practiced agriculture on any kind of wide scale, yet they lived in established villages, undertook colossal building projects, and participated in trade networks spanning thousands of miles. The cornerstone of this prosperity—the calories that fueled their prosperity—were fish species found in and around Florida's mangroves. (*Florida Museum of Natural History*)

Perhaps the greatest testament to the success of Florida's mangrove-based societies are the tremendous temple mounds that line the Gulf Coast. Composed on a foundation of sand and shells, rising up out of the mangrove forests, these mounds tower dozens of feet overhead even after a millennium of settling, erosion, and hurricanes. They stand as a powerful demonstration to the affluence of the peoples who, a 1,000 years ago, could muster the substantial manpower required to erect and maintain these hulking structures—which would have been hard to come by in a subsistence-level society.

Mound Key, shrouded by vast mangrove forests in Estero Bay, is believed to have been the seat of Calusa power for 500 years. To facilitate canoe traffic at their capital—to aid in the passage of fishermen and merchants—laborers constructed a grand canal, some 2,000 feet in length and approximately 100 feet wide. They also devised sophisticated watercourts—watery enclosures adjacent to the mangroves—into which they drove or deposited schools of fish to live out their final days, awaiting an easy harvest before making landfall on the dinner plate of the Calusa elite.[2]

In 2001, 100 miles to the north of Mound Key in Tampa Bay, a fisherman named Harold Koran discovered the 40-foot remnants of a canoe submerged in the mud and muck on the edge of a mangrove forest. Radiocarbon dating suggests that this canoe dates to a period between 690 and 1010 CE. Aside from some rot—and a bit of damage from a few persistent mangrove prop roots growing directly through its hull—it is remarkably well preserved for its age. Archeologists believe this canoe—the largest ever found in Florida—was originally in excess of 45 feet in length, with a raised prow designed to traverse the open waters of the bay, or possibly even the Gulf of Mexico.[3]

From the artifacts that they left behind, we know that the Weeden Island Culture that produced this canoe—and its far more powerful Calusa neighbors to the south—were part of an active trade network extending in relay to the American Midwest, to Cuba, maybe even to the Yucatan. The canoe was something like an ancient semi-truck—facilitating exchange between this prosperous coastal society and trading partners up and down Florida's Gulf Coast.

This vessel, abandoned for unknown reasons, was protected by the mangrove forest around it for 1,000 years, shielded from wave and tidal action that might otherwise have broken it up or swept it out to sea. Similarly, the anaerobic conditions of the soil around it—packed in place by the prop roots and pneumatophores of the forest—may even have inhibited its rate of decomposition. It grants us a window into an ancient, lost world, inhabited by people who understood how to harvest the abundance of the mangroves—who understood that they owed their relative affluence to the ecosystems branching out from these incredible trees.

This close relationship continued unabated until the arrival of Europeans in the sixteenth century. First contact with the Spanish was informal and poorly documented. The newcomers sought native slaves for their Caribbean plantations, then later, local riches in the vein of what they had found amidst the Mexica or the Inca. The Spanish were little impressed by what the Calusa or anyone else in Florida had built, commenting on their lack of gold and silver almost as often as they remarked on the locals' nakedness.[4]

"These Indians occupy a very rocky and a very marshy country. They have no product of mines," wrote Hernando de Escalante Fontaneda, survivor of a 1549 shipwreck off Florida's coast. He lived as a Calusa slave for seventeen years before his rescue, and his

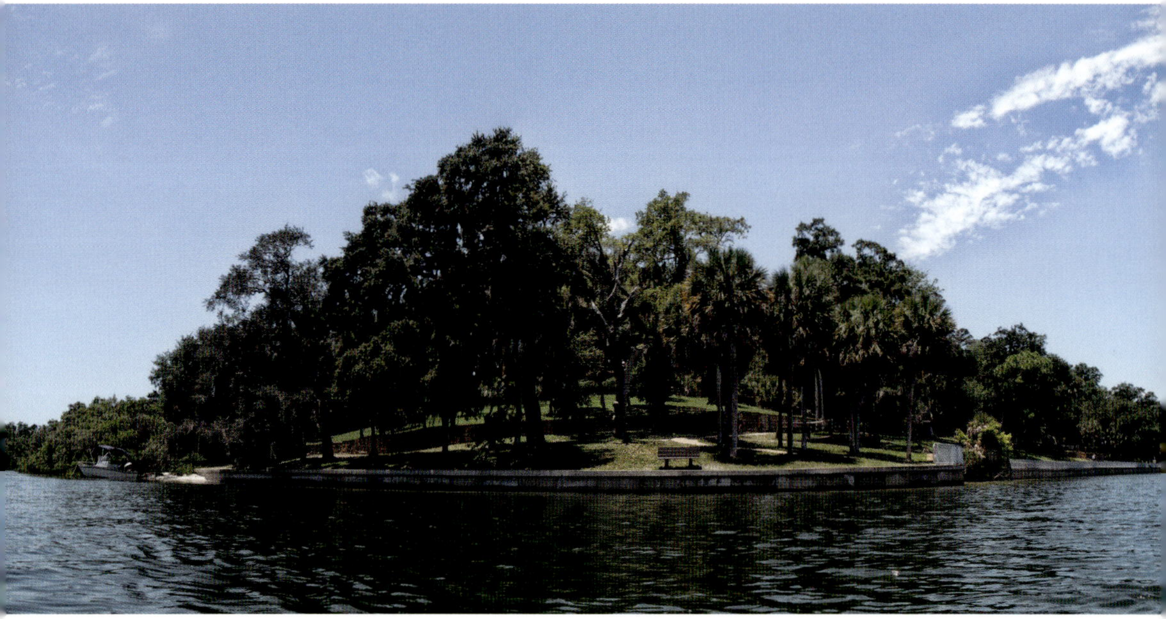

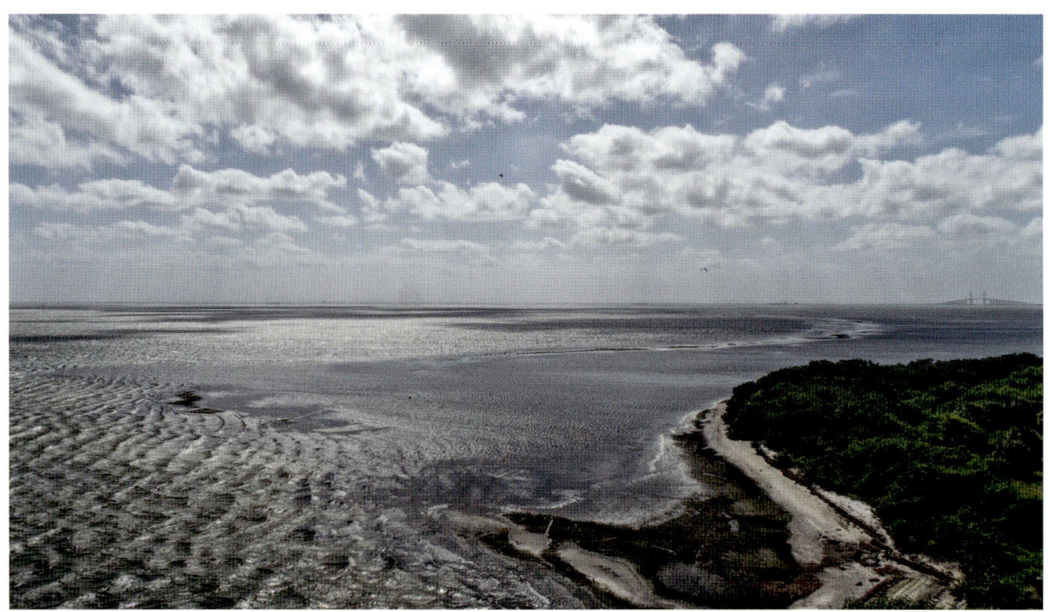

The Tocobaga Temple Mound—built entirely by hand beginning around a thousand years ago—is the largest surviving native mound in the Tampa Bay region. It lay at the center of an L-shaped village, which extended into rich mangrove habitat to the south and north. The village of Tocobaga was home to as many as 2,500 people when the Spanish first visited in the 1500s.

An expansive view of what was and what could be. Much of Florida's southern coastline looked this way at the time of Spanish contact. The peninsula would be better prepared for the coming challenges of climate change if it still did.

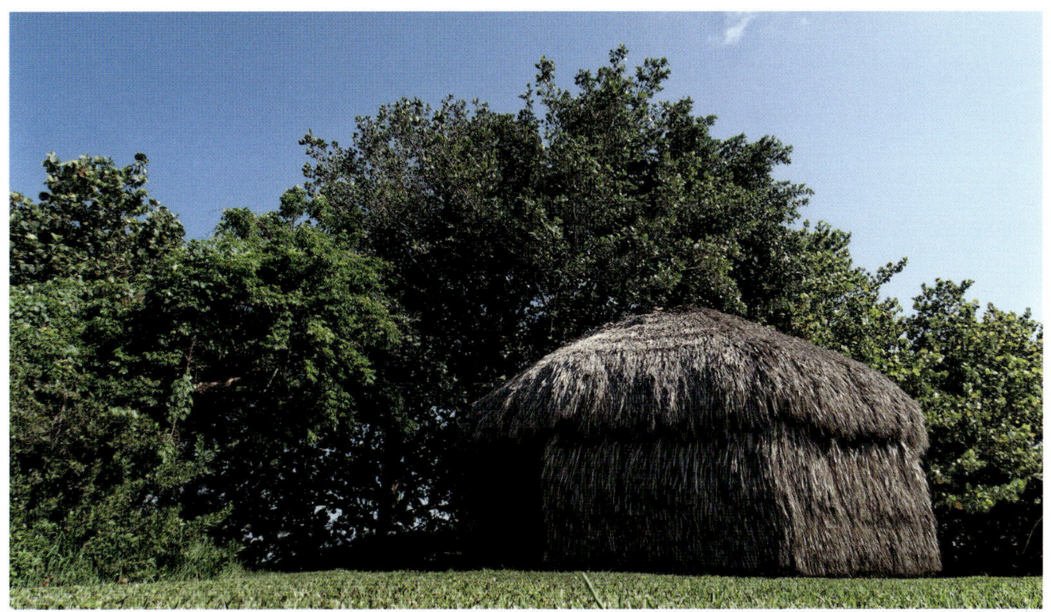

A reconstructed hut representing the Uzita village at De Soto National Monument on the south side of Tampa Bay. Archeology and written Spanish accounts demonstrate just how frequently the peoples of south Florida made their homes on very edge of lush mangrove forests—and how much their way of life revolved around these rich spaces.

1575 memoir of this experience is one of our most detailed eyewitness records of native life in coastal Florida. "The men go naked, and the women in a shawl made of a kind of palm-leaf, split and woven."

Lack of metal and clothing notwithstanding, Fontaneda goes on at length about the quality of the Calusa diet. Though he was disgusted by their habit of eating turtles and alligators, he remarked with approval about the foods that they extracted from the mangroves, writing about the prodigious amount of waterfowl that they ate and noting that "fish is plenty and very good."

The Spanish engaged in numerous skirmishes with these peoples—including the 1521 battle in which a poison-tipped Calusa arrow killed the famous Ponce de Leon. In fact, in many early encounters, Florida's natives—stout from their robust diet and fighting formidably on their home turf—often gained the upper hand. The greatest slaughter was unwitting, however—the Spanish carried Old World diseases against which the natives carried no herd immunity.

Native populations were decimated, their societies thrown into disarray. It was in the aftermath of this upheaval that later groups like the Seminole coalesced. The Seminole were relative newcomers to the Florida peninsula—the reconstituted, syncretic remnants of societies from across the Southeast, overturned by European contact—waging their own rearguard action against the advancing people of the United States.

As a consequence of all this tumult, carnage, and forced migration, so much of the cultural knowledge of Florida's earlier coastal peoples was lost. The Calusa and the

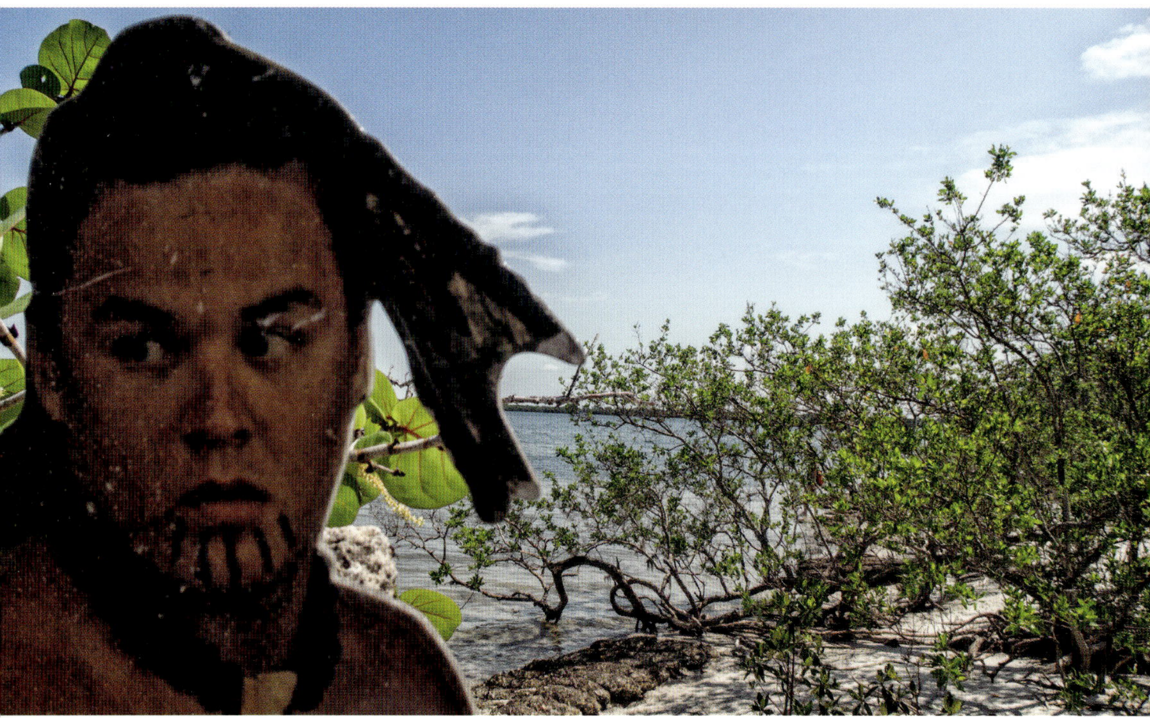

The native peoples of Florida were almost completely wiped out by Spanish contact, whether through direct acts of violence, the scourge of disease, or through broad political destabilization wrought by both. Much of their cultural and ecological knowledge was lost in the turmoil. (*Educational display at DeSoto National Monument*)

Manasota were not flawless societies—they waged their share of wars, demanded tribute from subjugated neighbors, and practiced their own forms of slavery and religious sacrifice. It is important not to romanticize them into some soft focus stereotype of the noble savage.

But at least one quality exhibited by these peoples should be of interest to anyone interested in a sustainable future for Florida: These native societies extracted value from the land and the sea. Yet, after millennia of occupation, they had still barely scarred the surface of Florida in any lasting way. A large part of their stupendous success lay in the way that they skillfully integrated themselves into the web of life woven through Florida's mangrove forests—maintaining an impressive standard of living without overdrawing from the ecosystems around them.

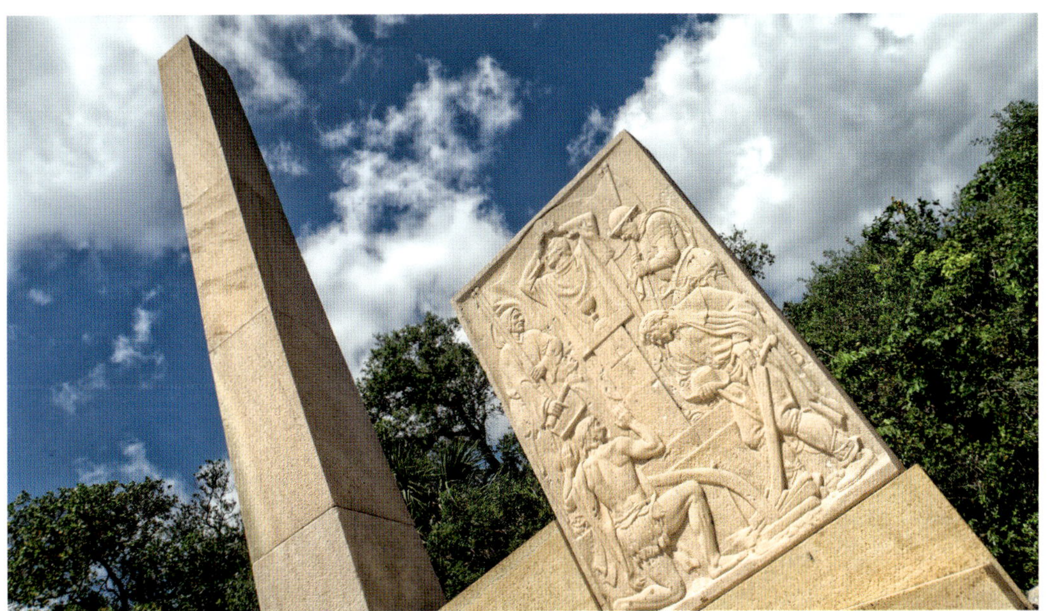

The Holy Eucharist Monument (above) and the Memorial Cross stand on county land just outside DeSoto National Monument. They are dedicated to De Soto, "Conquistador of the Faith" and to the twelve clergymen who accompanied him in 1539—a controversial marker in the shifting sands of Florida's history.

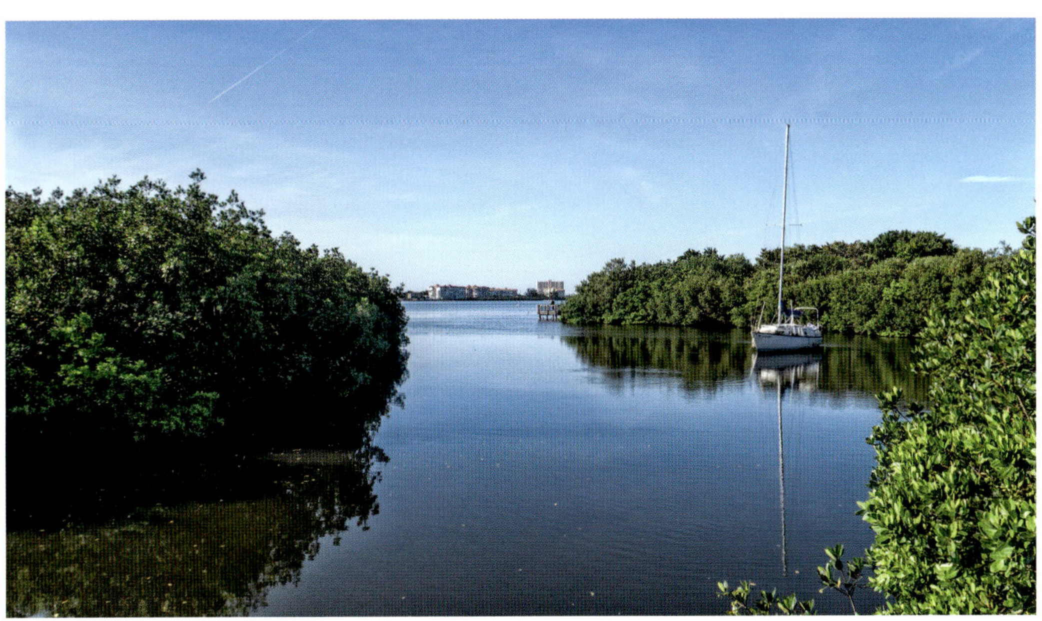

Throughout most of the twentieth century, the Clam Bayou estuary in Boca Ciega Bay was reshaped by humans. In the twenty-first century, a new generation of Floridians used their unique human talent for transformation in a fresh way, restoring dozens of acres to their natural state—as a thriving mangrove forest.

3

OF MEN AND MANGROVES

The Achilles heel of mangroves is that they're occupying that part of the landscape that people really covet.

Ilka "Candy" Feller
Emeritus scientist at the Smithsonian Environmental Research Center.[1]

Of course, the new Floridians continued to fish and otherwise harvest the bounty of Florida's waters—but the urge to remake Florida in the image of drier lands took precedence, accelerating in the middle years of the twentieth century as the state's population boomed. Most of these efforts to transform the landscape were couched in the notion of progress—a Florida Dream, a steady and rising tide that would lift all boats. Florida would be the East Coast analog of California—the Sunshine State, where the living was good, the weather was mild, and land was cheap.

Before the era of tourism and luxury resorts, Florida's economy was built around resource extraction, agriculture, and ranching. The peninsula's interior was mostly settled by cattle ranchers, turpentine producers, and phosphate miners. The coasts were claimed by fishermen whose footprint on the shore itself was limited. Antonio Maximo Hernandez, who maintained a fishing camp on the southern tip of the Pinellas peninsula as early as the 1830s, is emblematic of the nineteenth-century frontier fisherman—most of his time ashore was spent processing his catch and maintaining his equipment, not clearing mangroves.[2]

In the final decades of the nineteenth century, though, things were beginning to change. Florida—its natives now subdued—was advertised far and wide to have a moderate, healthful climate. Small coastal villages saw the first waves of Northern settlers arrive, seeking relief in the warmth of the sun for maladies such as asthma.

Waterfront property was fast becoming the most valuable commodity in this iteration of Florida's reinvention.

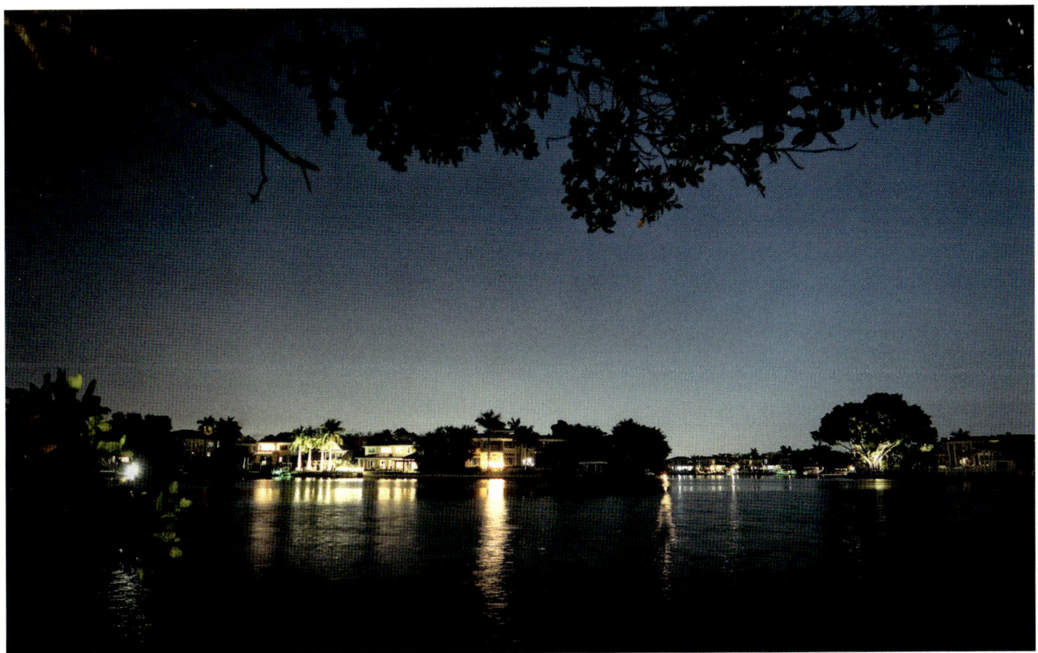

Twilight of the mangroves. So many of Florida's most desirable addresses, especially on the Gulf Coast, stand on land that was once mangrove forest—or else, they are built on fill dredged directly from the seafloor. Both techniques redraw the coastal map in ways that are disruptive to native mangrove habitats and the species that call them home.

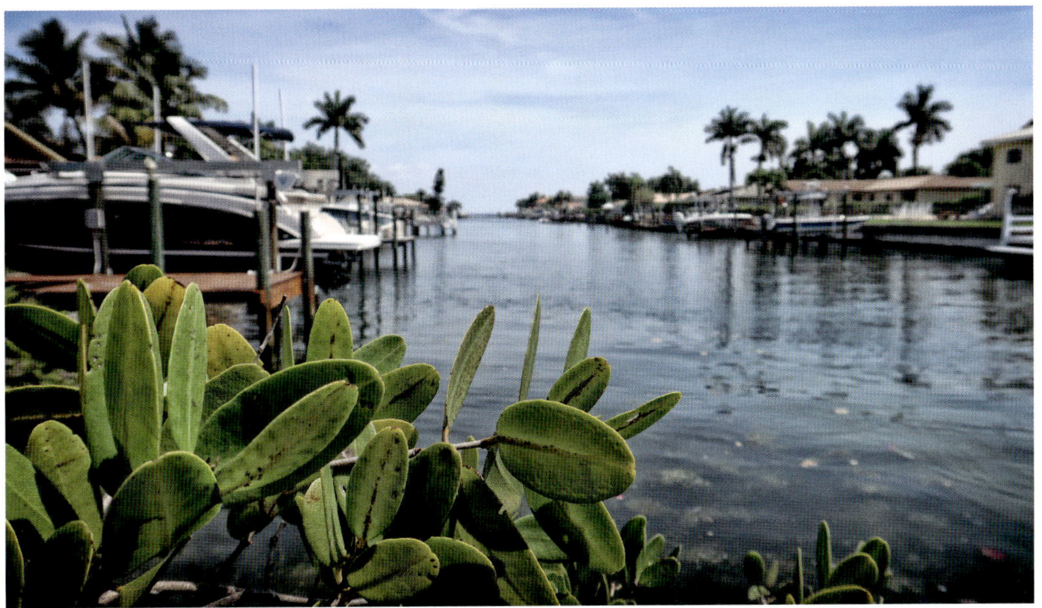

"When (Snell Isle), originally a muddy mangrove island, officially opened in October 1925, only 39 of its 275 acres were above the high tide line. Even so, Snell quickly sold over seven million dollars' worth of lots there."
- *Tampa Bay Magazine.*

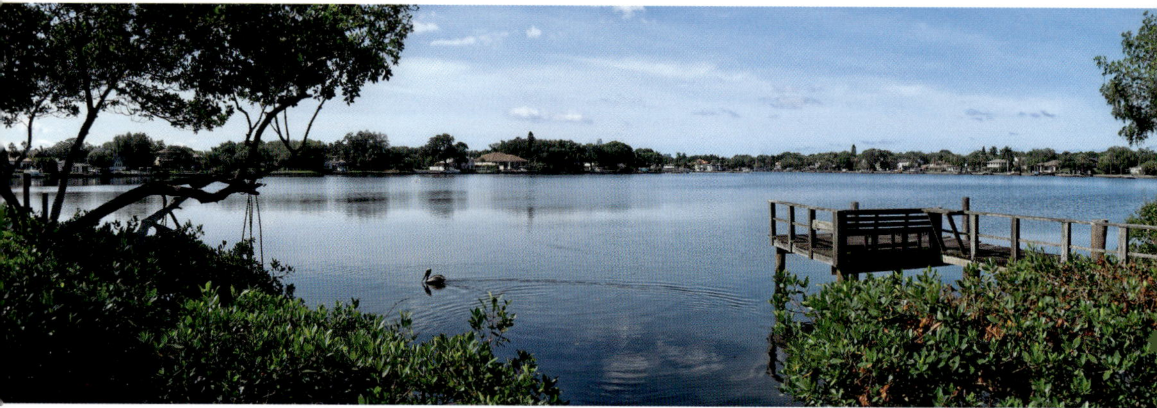

The red mangroves in the foreground have been trimmed to frame this placid view of Snell Isle in St. Petersburg. Today, it is almost as if the land calls out of that long-gone phantom forest—tidally-influenced sunny day floods are a common occurrence, and many streets are inches deep with standing water even when it has not rained.

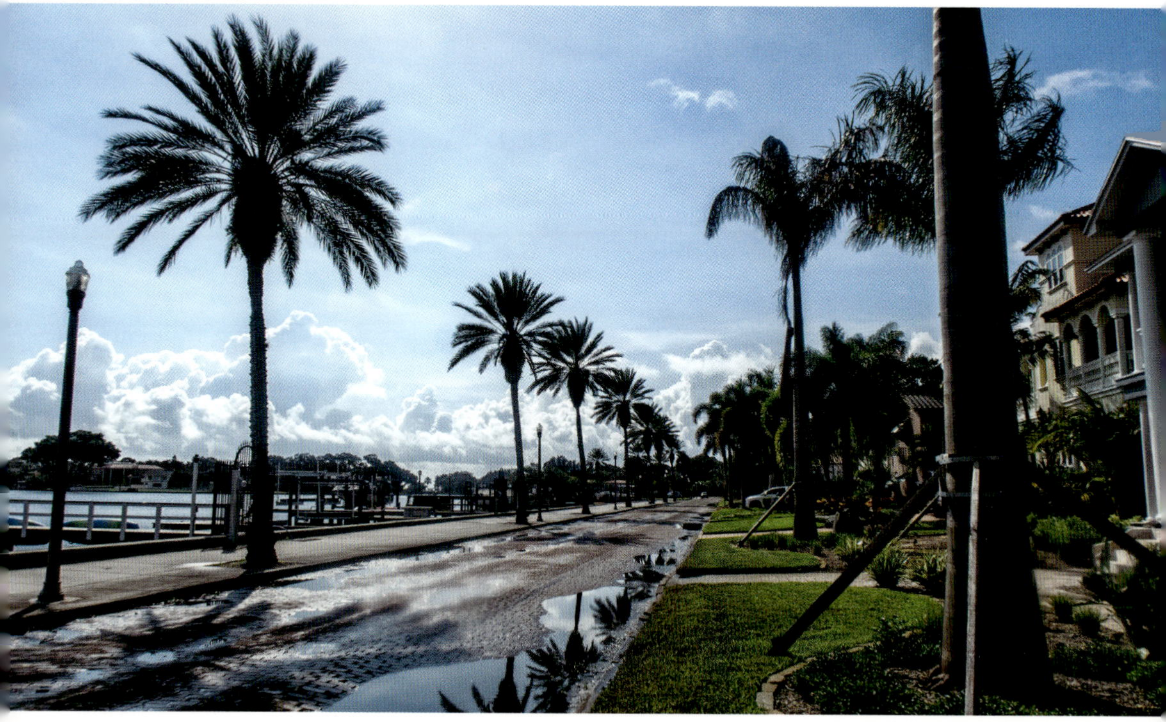

Sunny day flooding occurs in low-lying areas at high tide when seawater inundates gravity-fed sewer systems. The neighborhoods most impacted by this phenomena were often mangrove forests or salt marshes in a previous life. This type of flooding is indicative of even bigger problems not too far in the future, as ocean levels continue to rise.

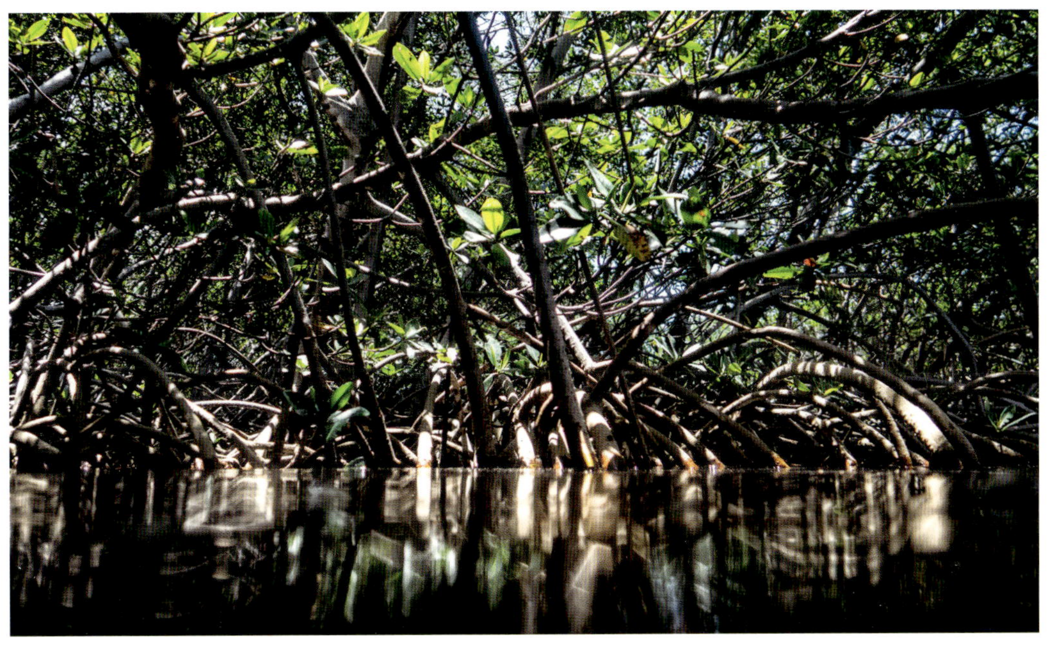

The "before" shot—what flooding and storm surge once meant along the Florida coast.

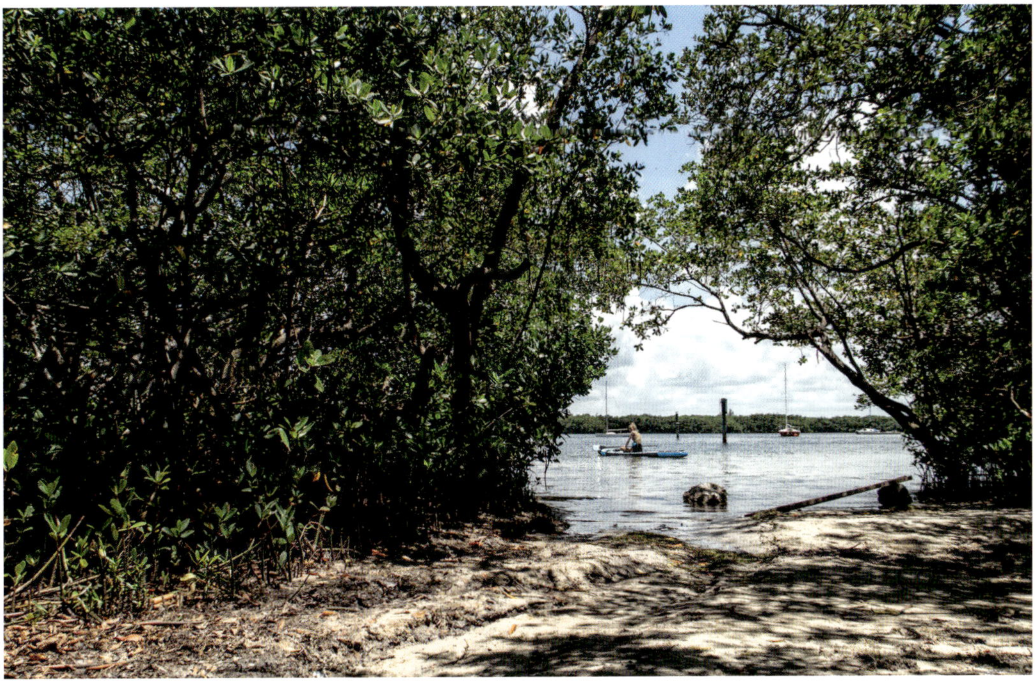

Recreation amidst the mangroves.

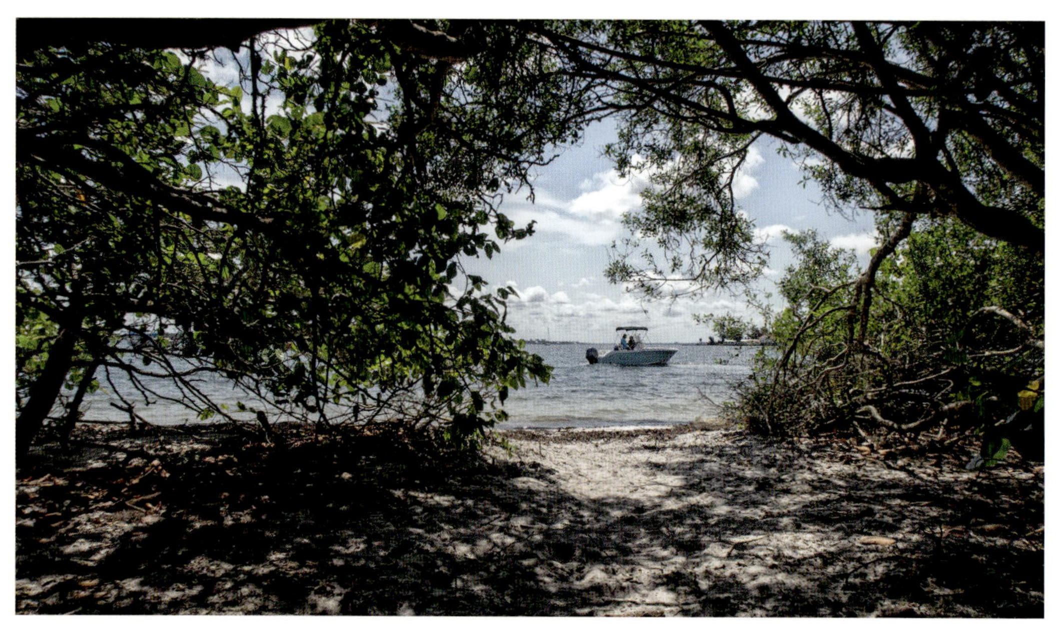

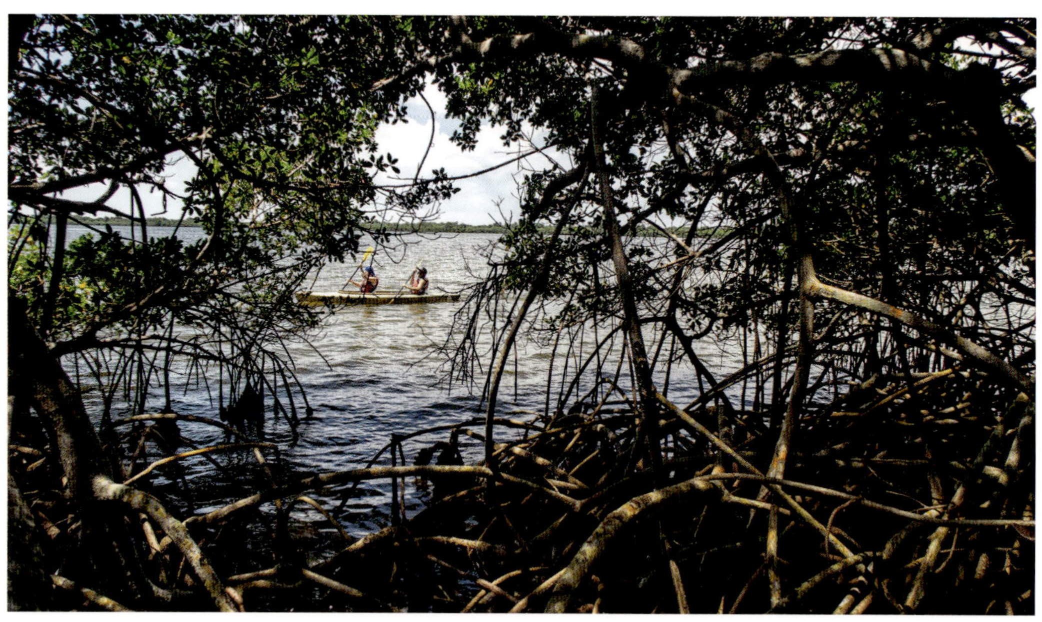

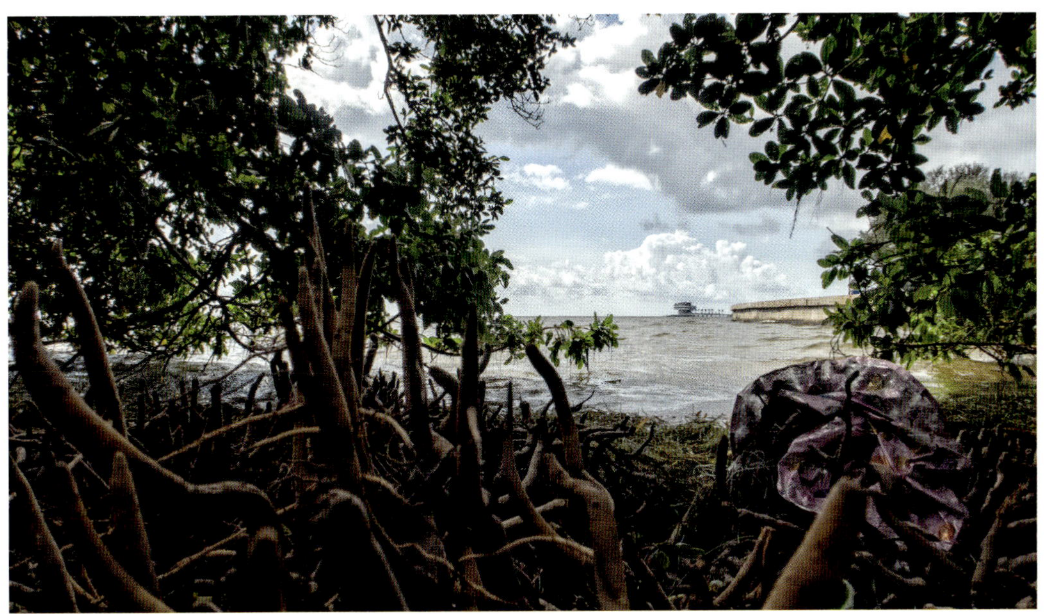

The party's over, but this Mylar balloon is sticking around. Nothing is ever really lost, and even with the best of intentions, no trash is ever disposed of with complete certainty. Mangroves catch more than their fair share of humanity's waste.

By the early years of the twentieth century, Florida's first residential real estate boom was on. Men like C. Perry Snell in St. Petersburg began to clear wide swathes of land—including vast mangrove forests—in order to build new luxury housing developments. A century later, his signature Snell Isle neighborhood is still one of the most desirable addresses in that city.[3]

Snell Isle was to be his "Pearl of Pinellas." Announcing the project in October 1925, Snell revealed his boundless ambitions as a real estate man—the swaggering confidence that he could improve upon nature and earn a pretty penny in the process.

"I see a vision of loveliness. Domes and towers will hold sway…. Romantic vision of lagoons…. Laughing waters amid flowers in bloom and the waving palms…. It may even approach the vistas of Paris," Snell wrote at a time when Snell Isle was home to far more mangroves than men.[4]

The story of Snell Isle is representative of countless other neighborhoods all along Florida's coastline. Over the last century, residential development has proven to be one of the primary drivers of mangrove habitat loss.

It is telling that the term "mangrove forest"—used elsewhere in this book in reference to a grove of the trees, as well as the unique biome that thrives in their midst—is synonymous with the less flattering phrase "mangrove swamp." Throughout most of the twentieth century—as humans developed the capacity to transform their earthly surroundings on an unprecedented, industrial scale—mangroves were broadly regarded as a nuisance or as an impediment to economic development. They were unproductive land, a barrier between here and the beach, a place to be filled

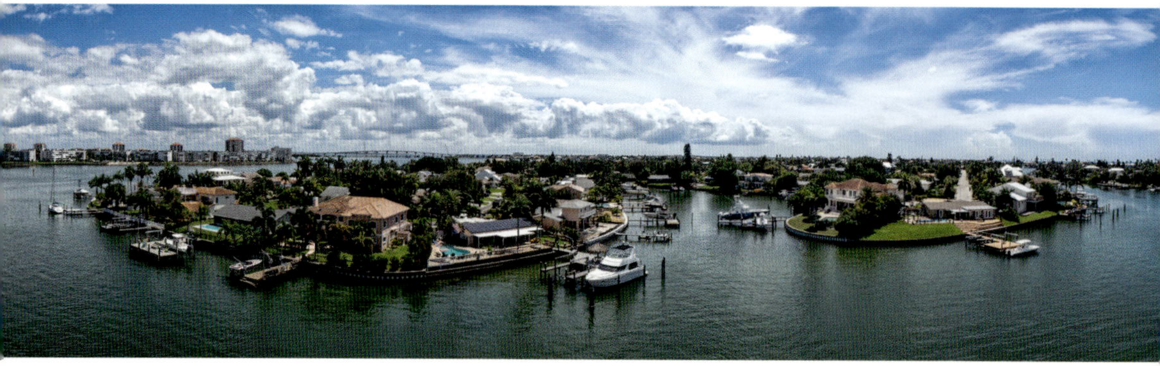

In Florida, your dreams can come true! Islands like these are artificial, the product of dredge and fill operations popular in the 1950s and 1960s. Held in place by concrete seawalls, these new islands are inhospitable to mangroves.

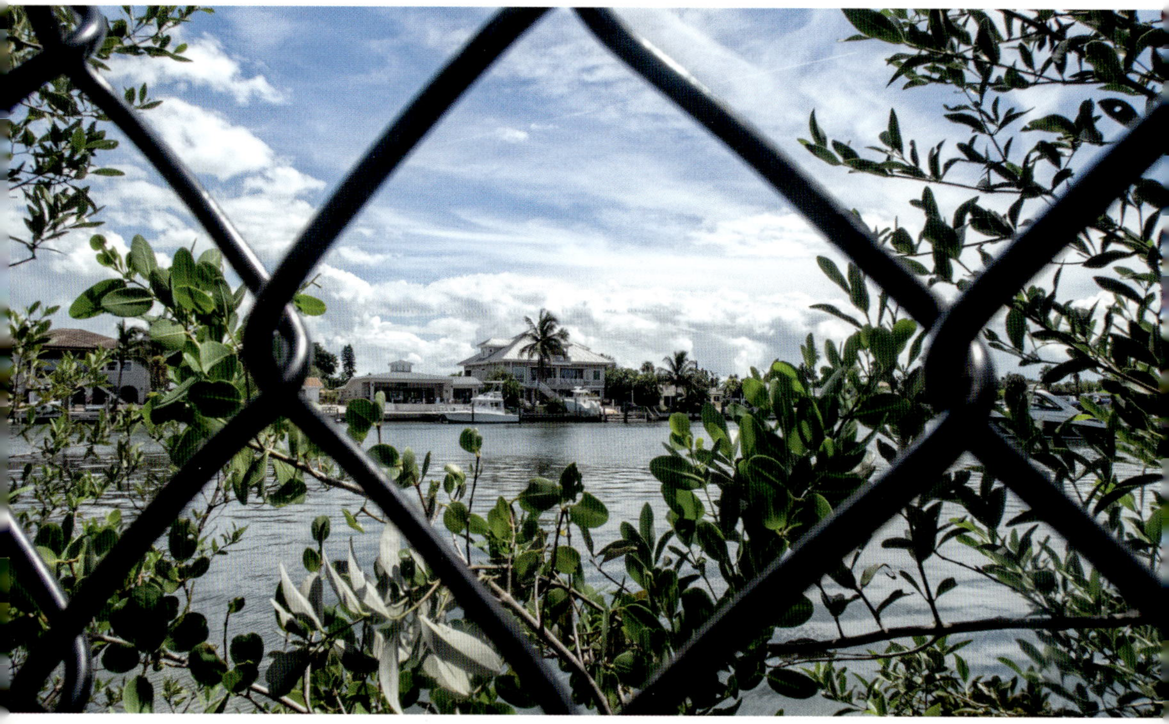

Can we reimagine waterfront neighborhoods like this one to better incorporate native habitats? Can we renegotiate what constitutes a beautiful view if it means a healthier community for every human, plant, and animal for miles around?

and dredged to make the most valuable commodity of all—another saleable parcel of land.

With that mindset, through the first three quarters of the 1900s, the fate of mangrove forests across the state followed a fairly predictable arc. Almost as a matter of policy, mangroves were felled and filled in, cut off from natural water cycles, which linked them to surrounding ecosystems, or in other ways disrupted—to stifle mosquito populations, to facilitate industry, and to make life more hospitable for the surging population that crowds Florida's coastlines today.

In a nation where the value of unspoiled nature is often calculated against the quarterly return on investment of extracting any saleable resources it may harbor, Florida's policy of swapping men for mangroves is almost uniquely shortsighted. And to make matters worse, this balance sheet is unfairly weighted in favor of an unsustainable quo by specific policy decisions made in Washington, D.C.

It seems obvious on the face of it that building homes in low-lying and flood-prone areas is a financially dubious proposition.

But one might argue that informed individuals have the right to assume such risks—living near the water is pleasant, and if you have the money to afford it, it should be your risk to assume. And that would be a fair point if the financial risk assumed were proportionately shouldered by the individuals moving into these neighborhoods.

However, in the United States, federal flood insurance and disaster relief have encouraged an unsustainable pattern of construction, which by extension has created conditions amenable to the historic loss of wetlands such as mangroves.

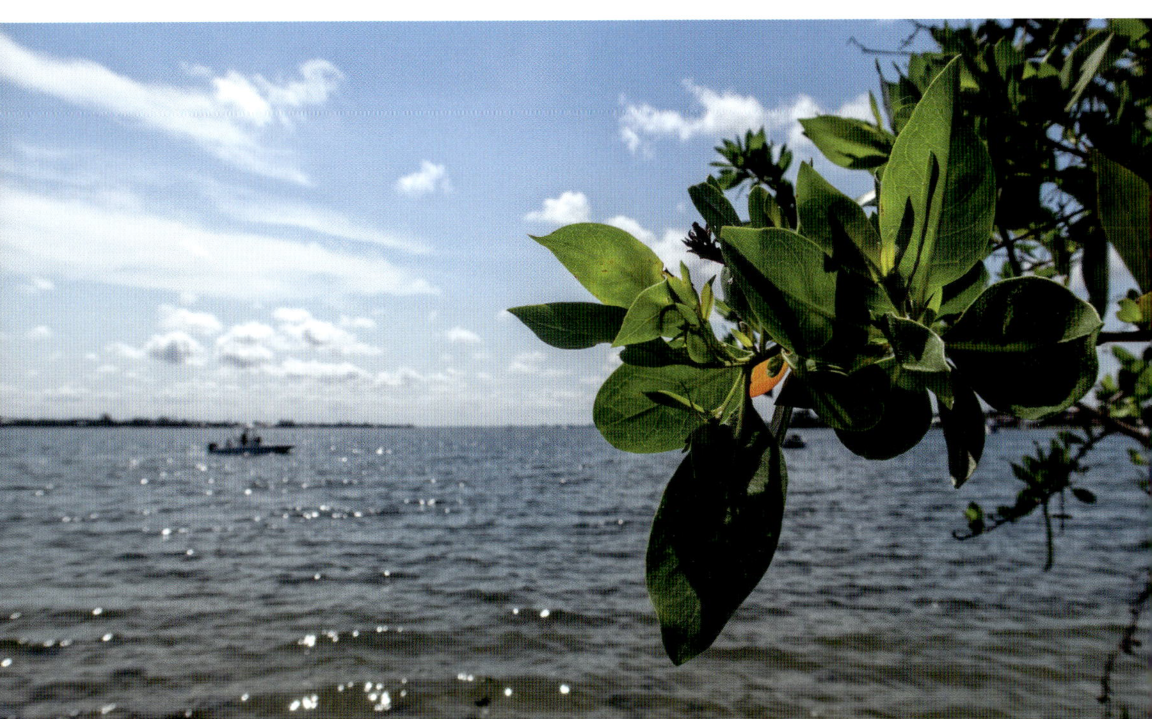

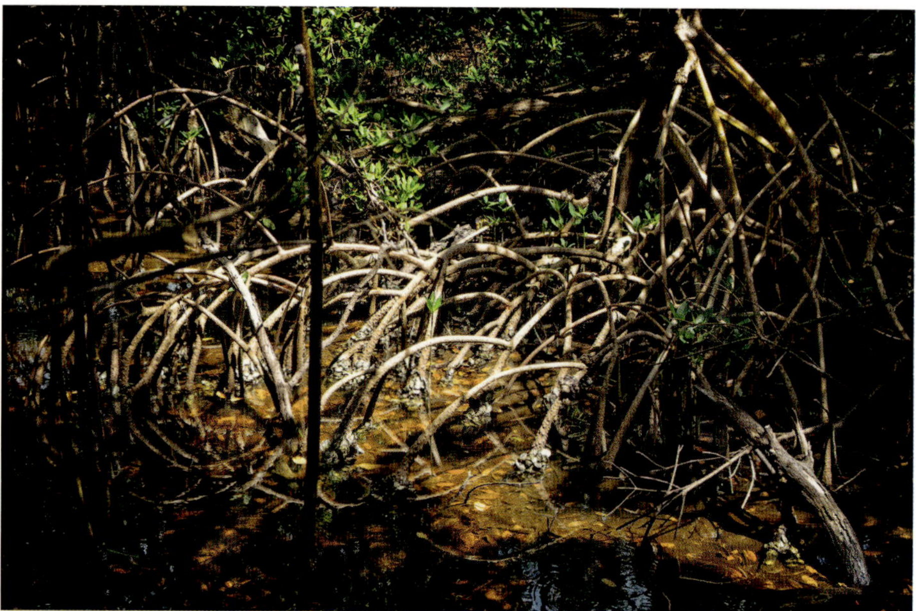

The female *Aedes sollicitans* mosquito lays her eggs within mangrove forests and salt marshes in depressions that dry out between periods of very high tide. Five days after these depressions are finally inundated, the eggs will hatch. To combat these pests, vast swathes of Florida's mangrove forests have been impounded—cut off from the tides, with disastrous effects for the many species of fish who spawn within.

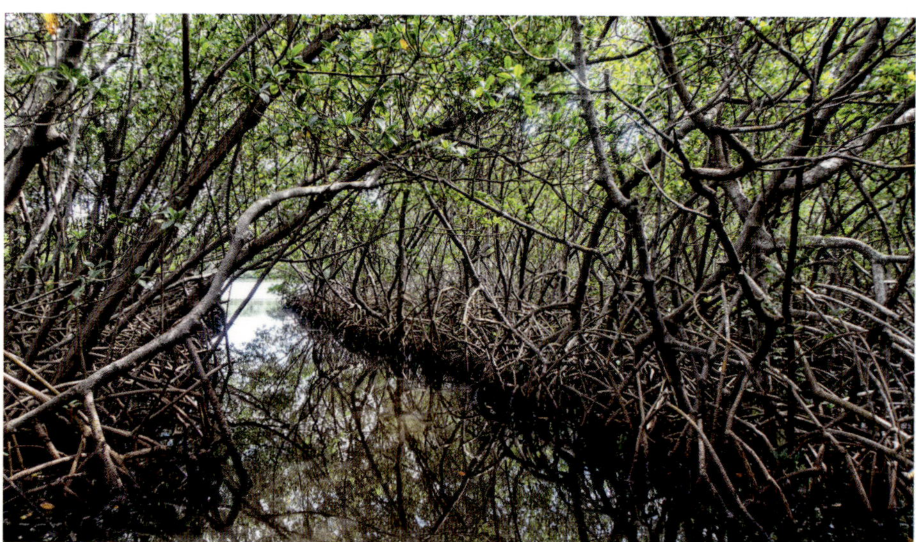

A ditch cleared through the mangrove forest as part of mosquito impoundment. Surveys around impounded forests showed dramatic declines in fish population and diversity. By the mid-1970s, some 40,000 acres of mangrove forest had been carved up this way. Some impoundments are actively managed to this day, while others have been left to revert to their natural state.

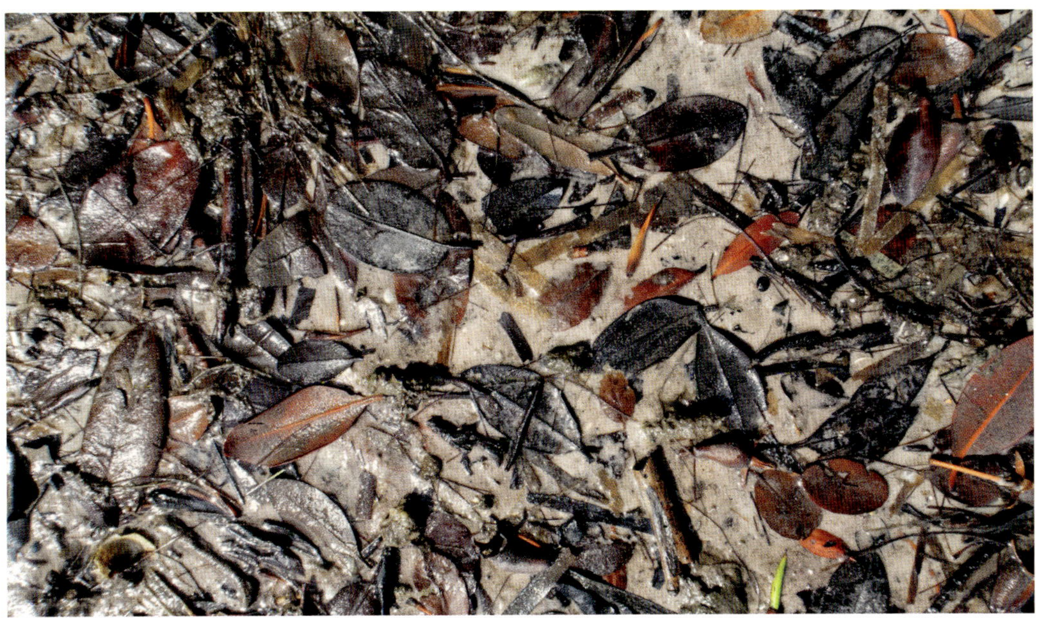

The wide array of detritus lining the floor of a mangrove forest—leaves, twigs, and animal waste—feeds a robust community of fungi. In a healthy forest, these fungi help to break down this organic matter so that it can be reabsorbed by plants and animals in and around the forest. It is a complete cycle that sequesters or recycles more carbon than is released into the atmosphere.

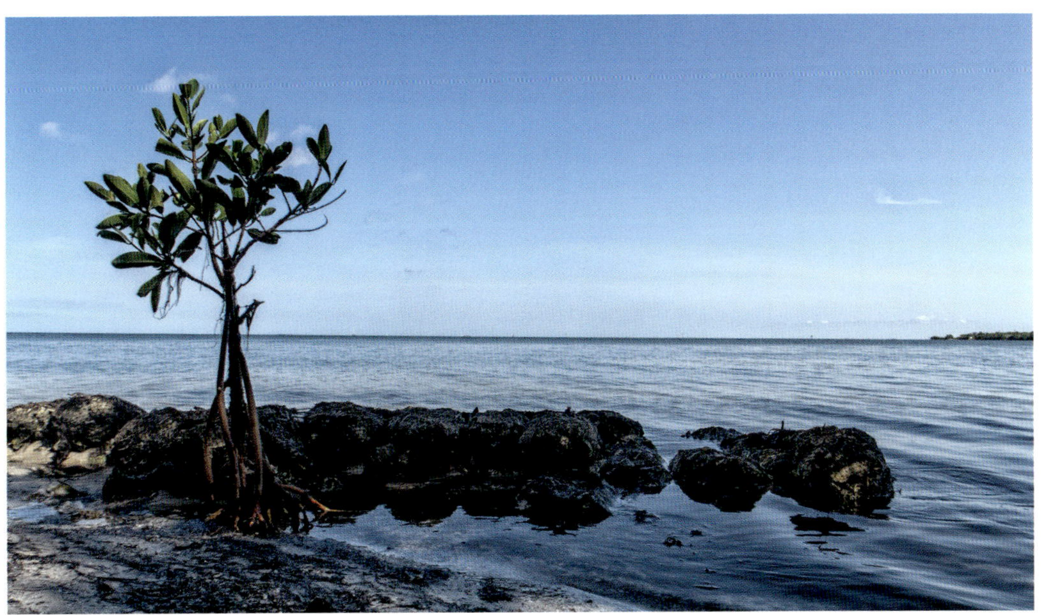

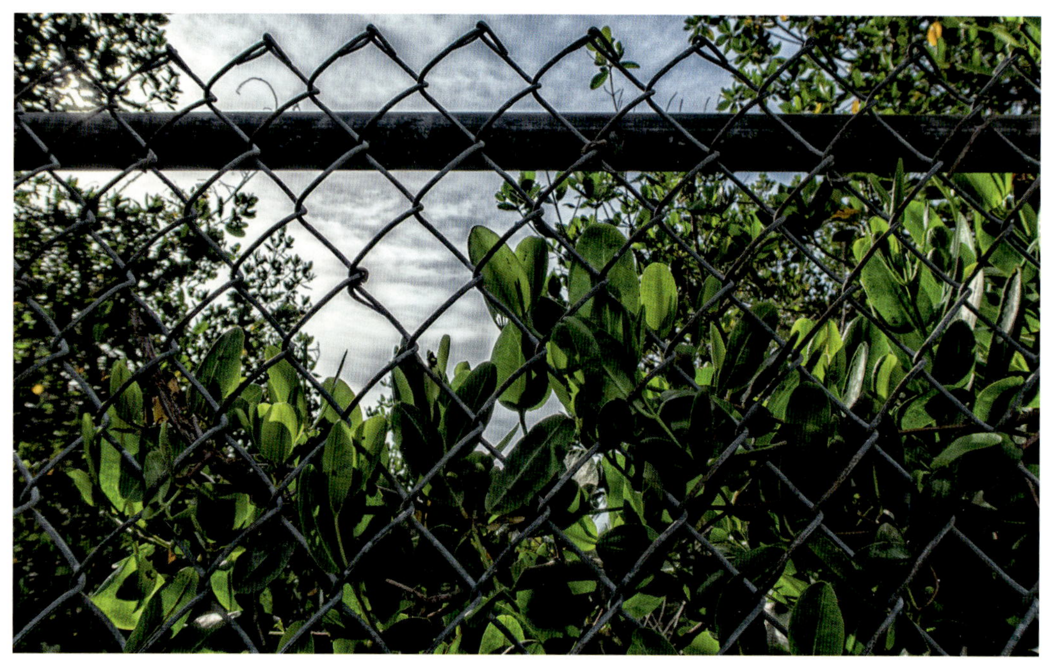

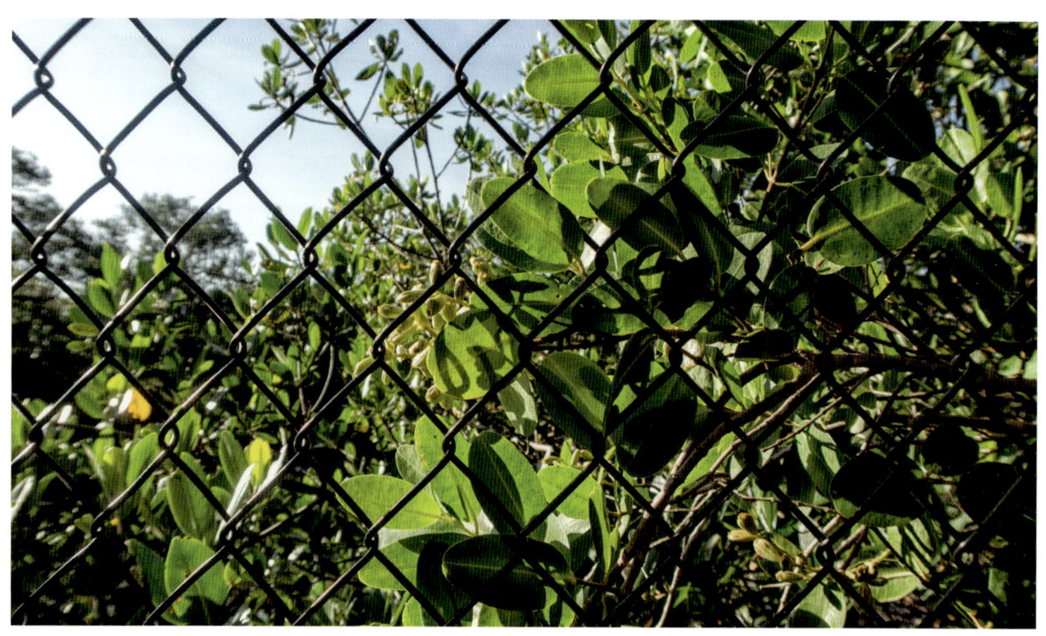

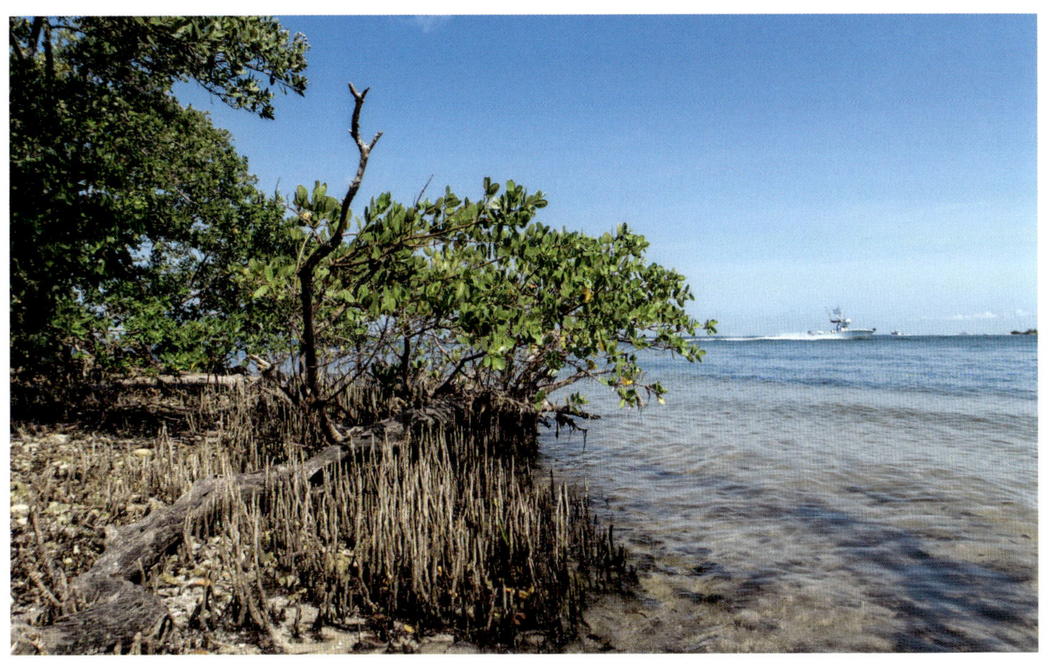

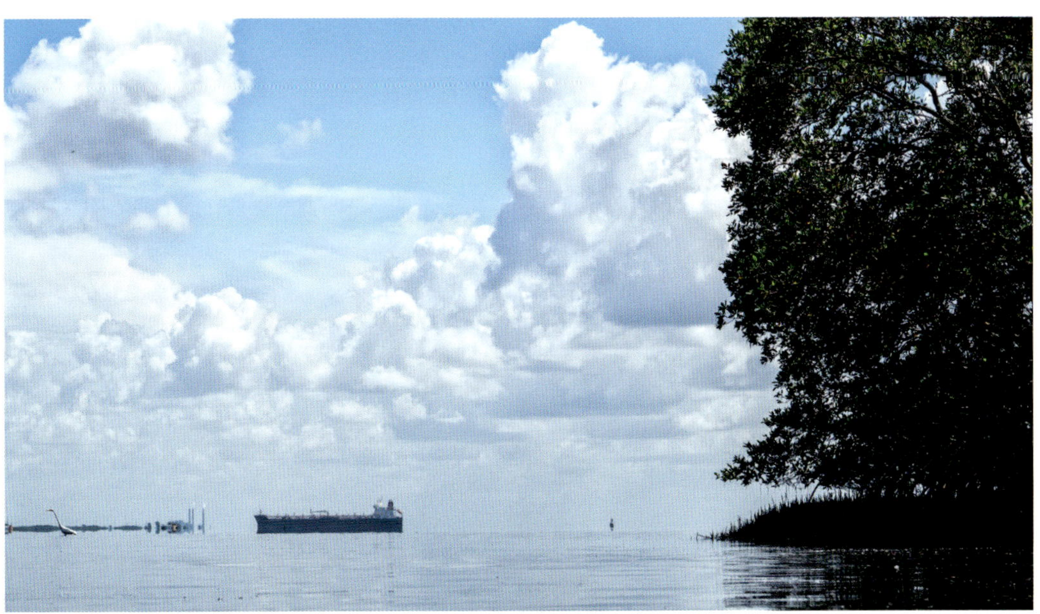

A container ship navigates the shipping channel near a vast mangrove forest. In order to accommodate a ship of this considerable draft and beam, such channels—gradually filled in by currents and other forces—must periodically be dredged.

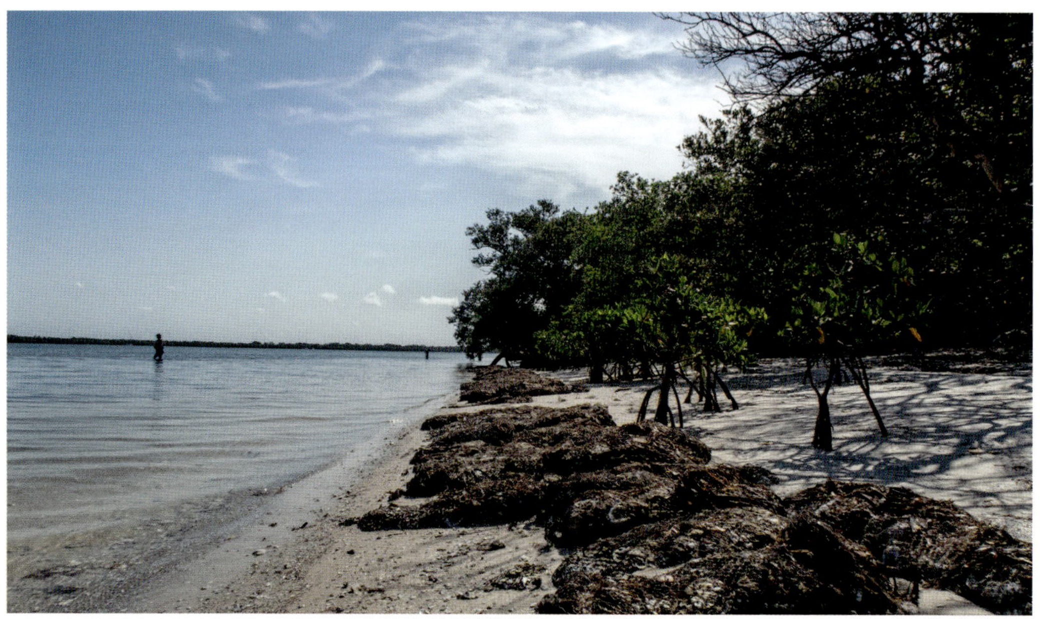

All beaches are subject to the forces of coastal erosion. Loose sand is swept out to sea by currents, wave action, storm surge, and heavy human traffic. This beach at DeSoto National Monument in Bradenton provides human access to the water—while protecting the shore from the most dramatic of these impacts.

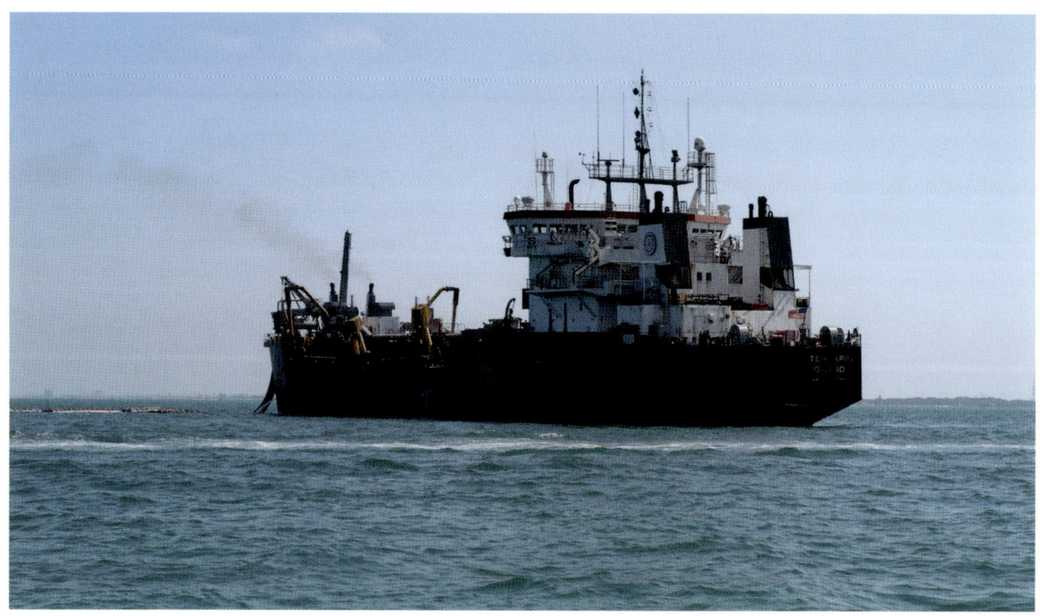

This ship draws a slurry of sand and seawater from the ocean floor, pumping it through a length of conduit to a nearby beach. Dredging can have a dramatic impact on nearby mangroves, and impact assessments and mitigation plans are now required before any such project.

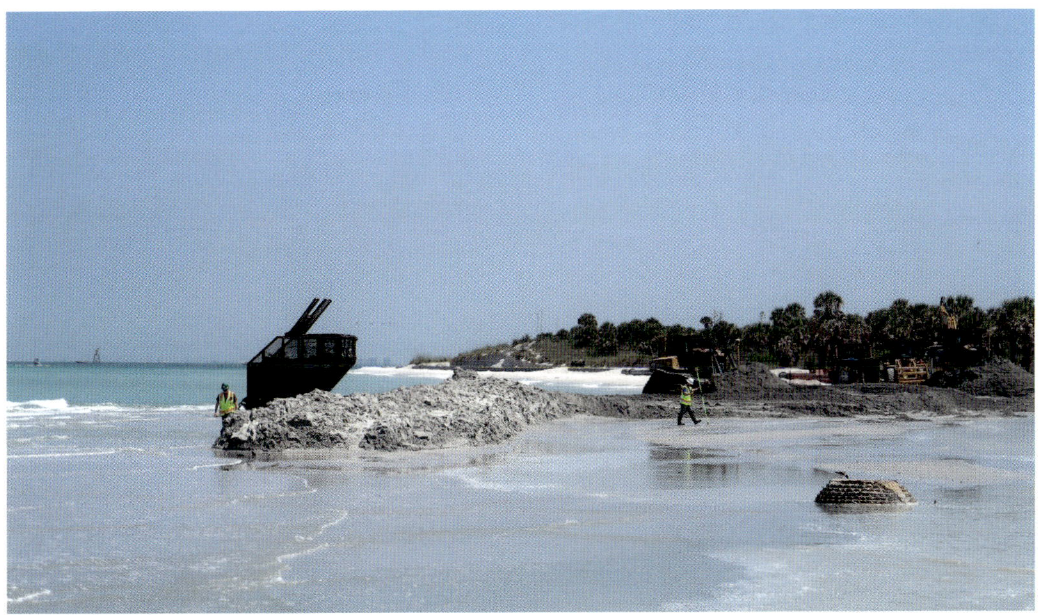

Workers mimic the natural distribution of sand on the shore, completing the process known as beach nourishment. This endeavor is both labor and capital intensive—and must be repeated on a regular basis. Coastal erosion is a natural phenomenon of concern to humans largely because the unstable waterfront has been deemed valuable property.

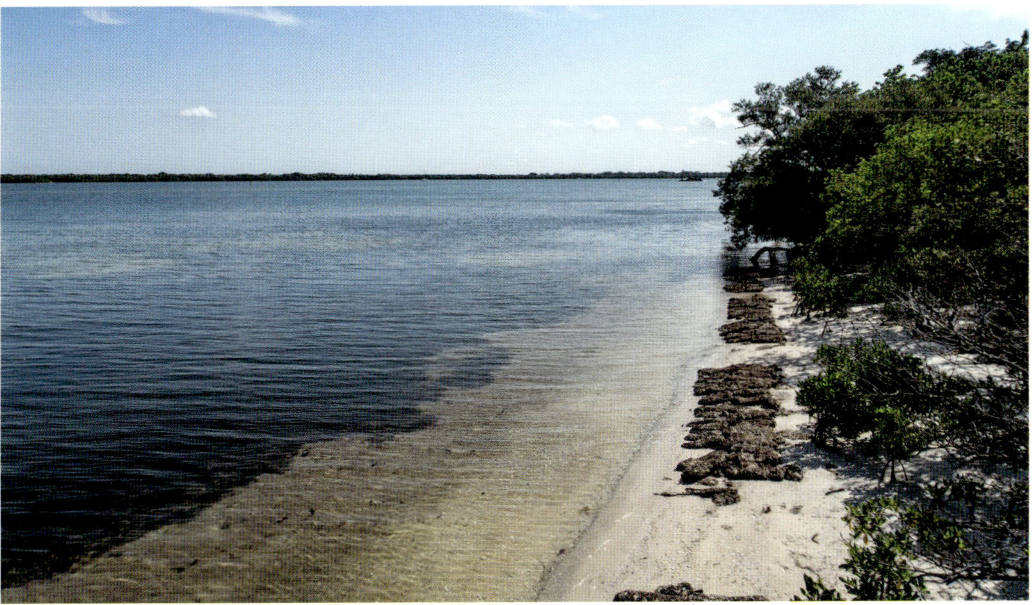

Between 1995 and 2001, Florida, in cooperation with the Army Corps of Engineers, spent $212 million on beach nourishment. Where currents and wave action are amendable, a more sustainable countermeasure against coastal erosion might involve a partial reintroduction of mangrove forests. What if more beaches looked like this one?

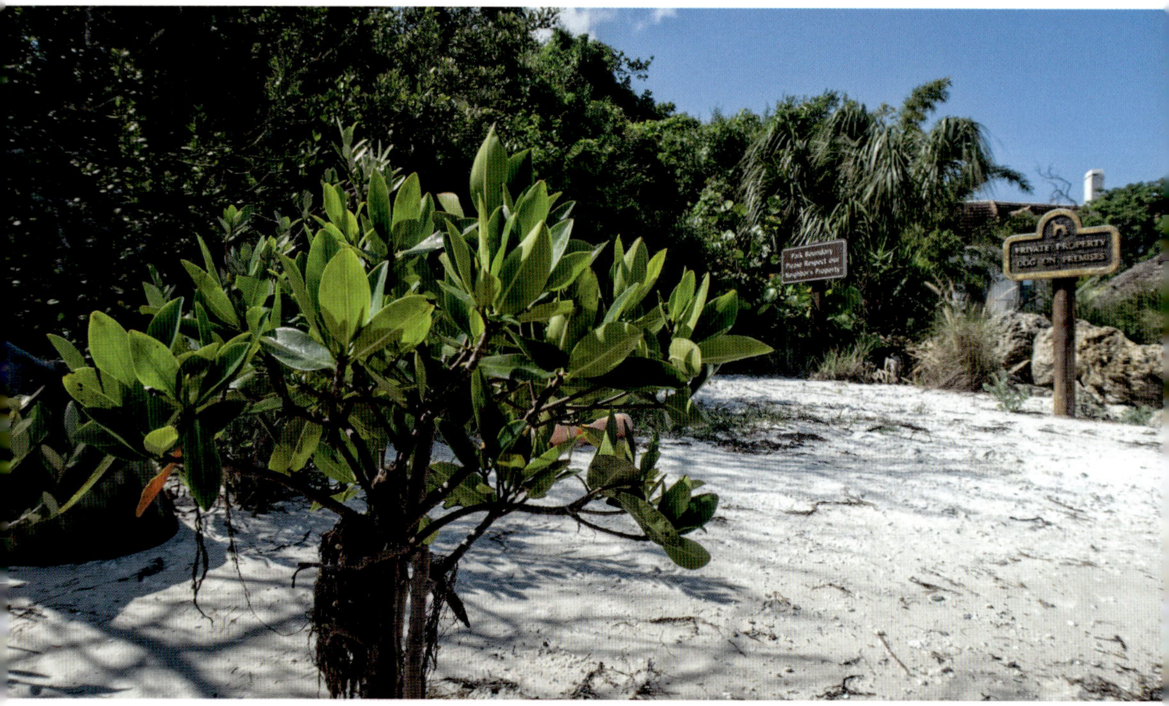

Pick a side—does the relationship between man and mangrove have to be such a stark line in the sand?

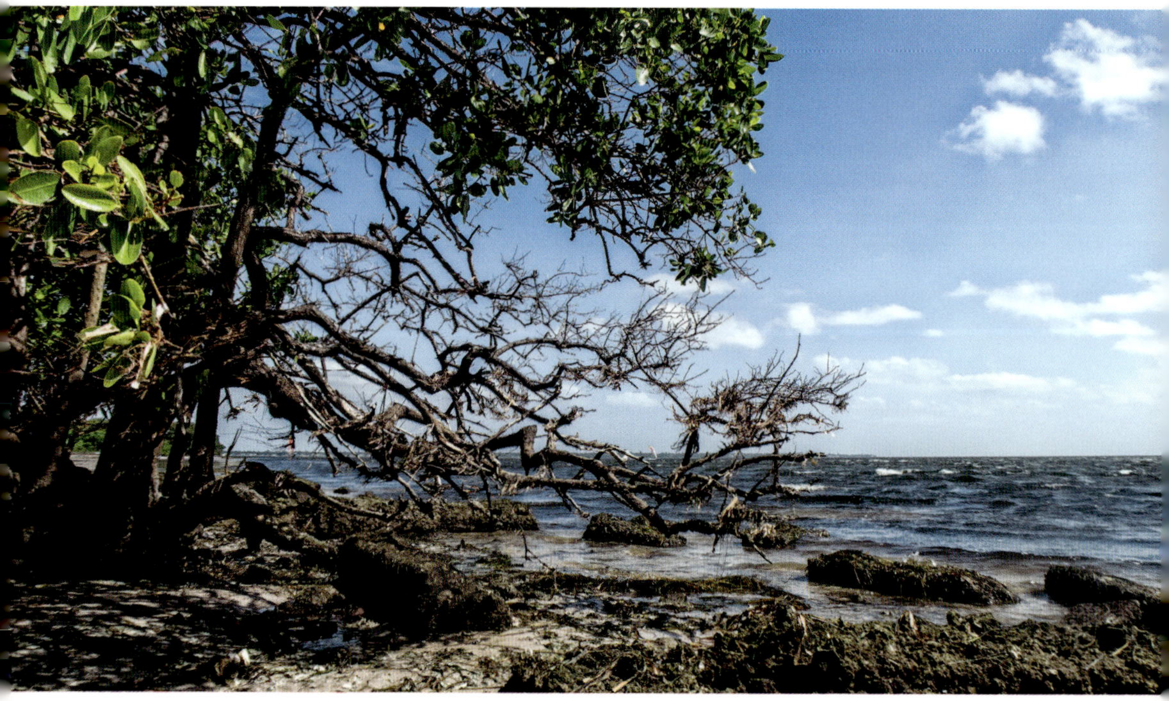

A white mangrove under some level of stress.

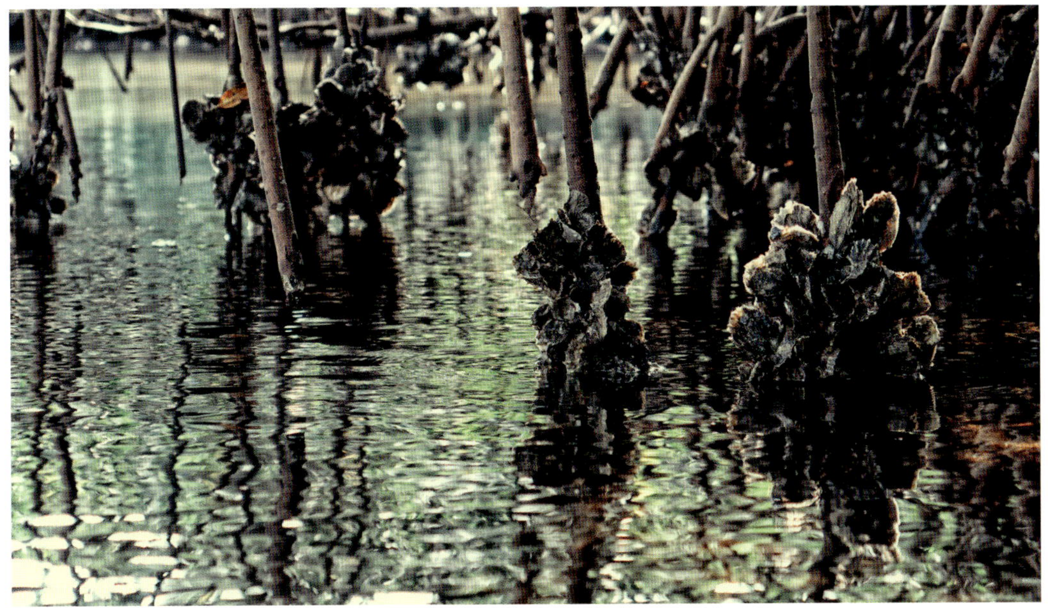

Oysters cling to the prop roots of a red mangrove. A single oyster can filter between 2 and 5 gallons of seawater per hour, removing sediment, algae, pollutants, bacteria, and even viruses while improving the overall health of the surrounding ecosystem.

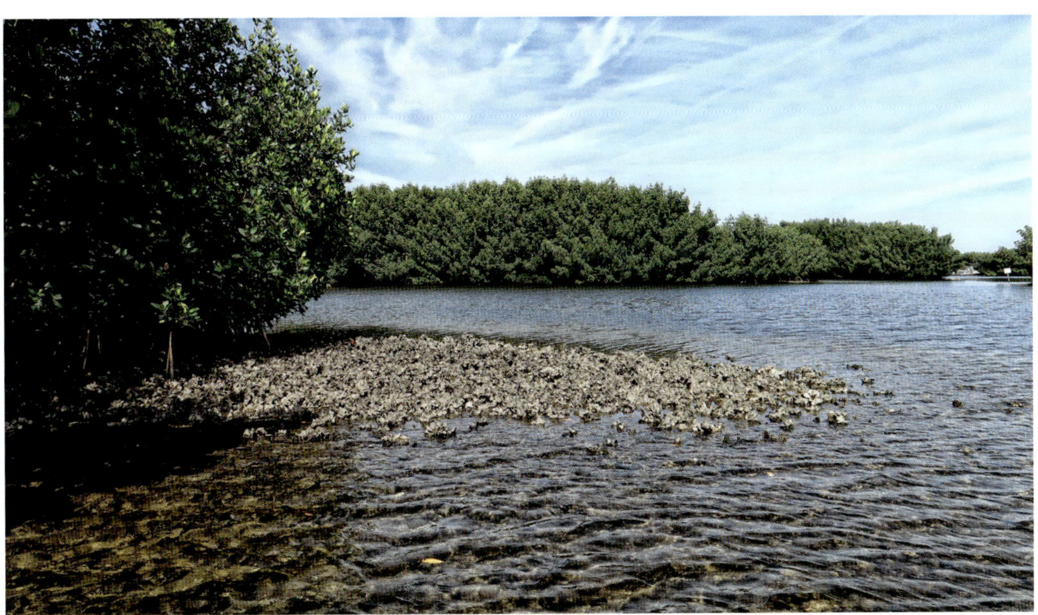

Oysters are known to colonize the firm substrate around mangroves, forming a structure known as a mangrove apron, or fringe reef. Taken together, these two species can create an incredibly stable barrier against waves and surge in one direction and erosion in the other—the ultimate self-maintaining seawall.

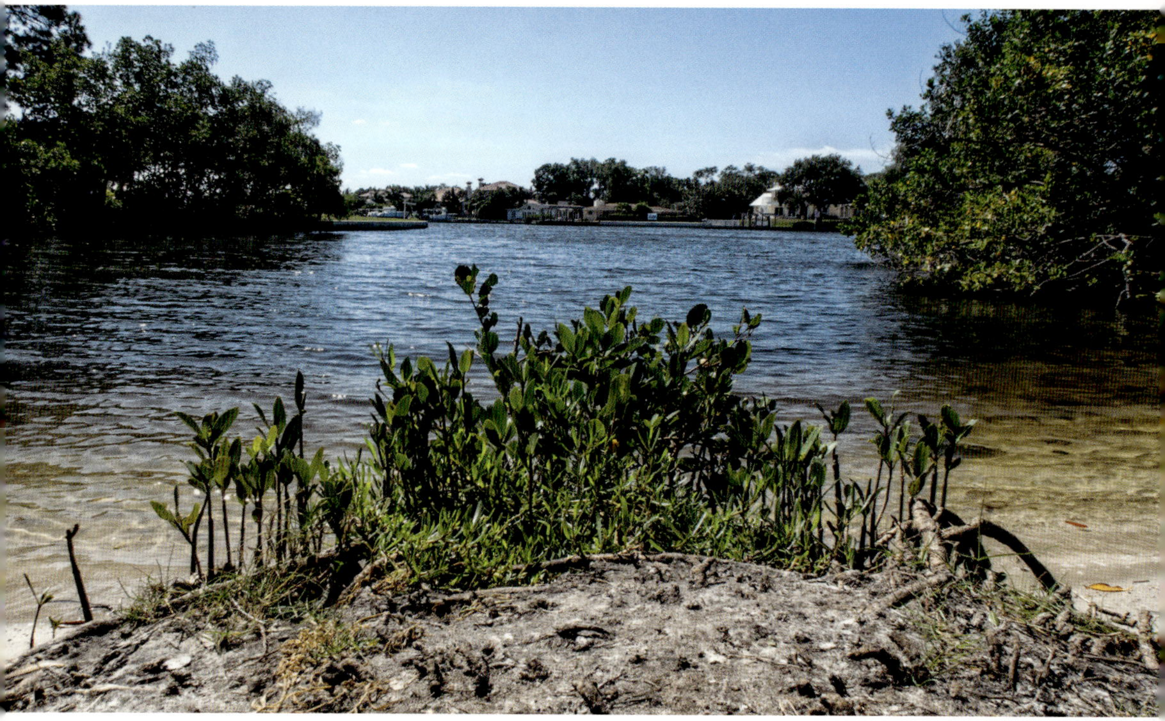

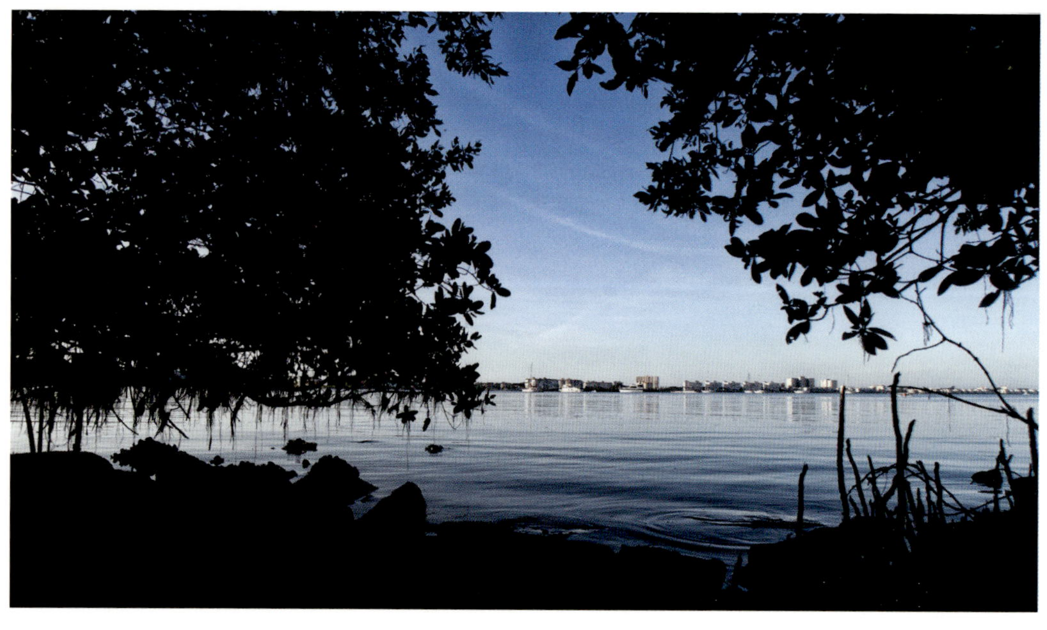

A new generation of mangroves takes hold in a neighborhood park—in their ancestral home. Who needs a seawall or riprap? Who needs a dredge?

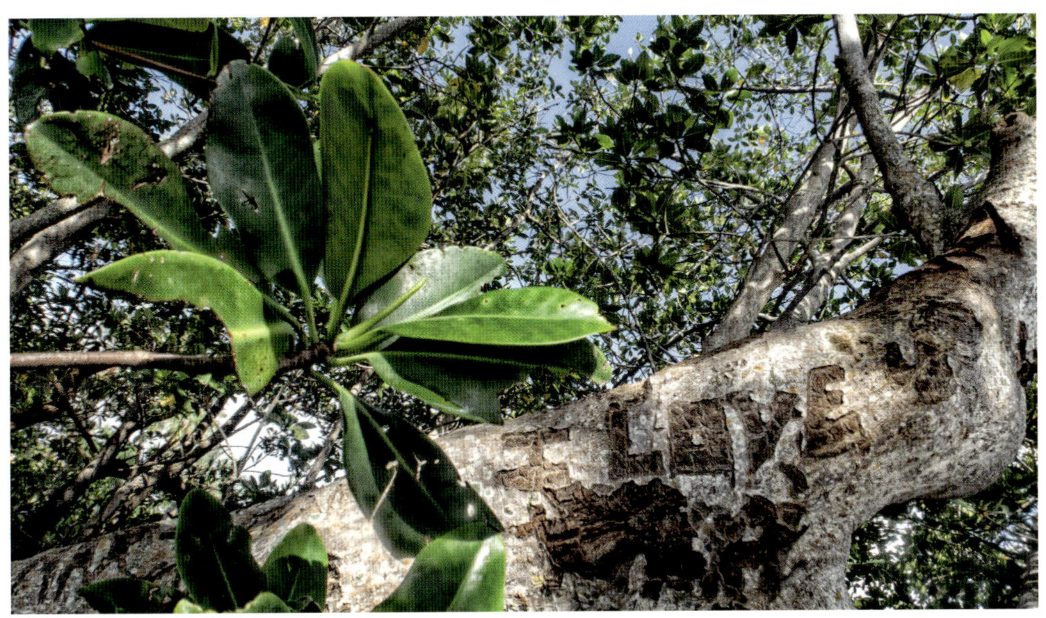

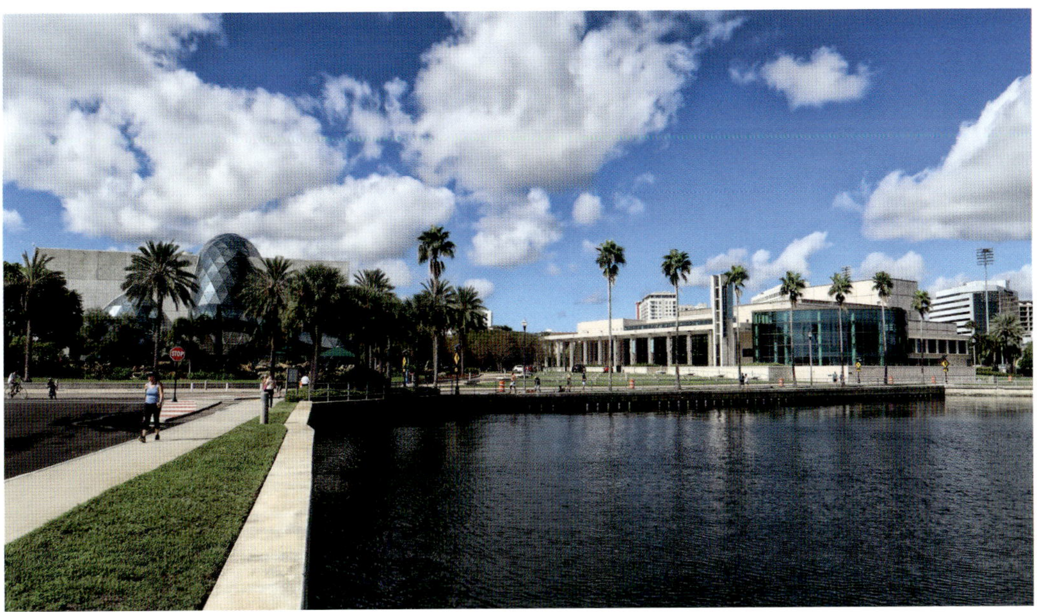

Dredge and fill along the waterfront in St. Petersburg—this photo was taken in a spot that was open water within living memory. There is almost no native vegetation in sight in this former wetland. Seawalls clearly serve a purpose, improving our quality of life when deployed judiciously—but as with so many things humans do, the question is always, "When is enough enough?"

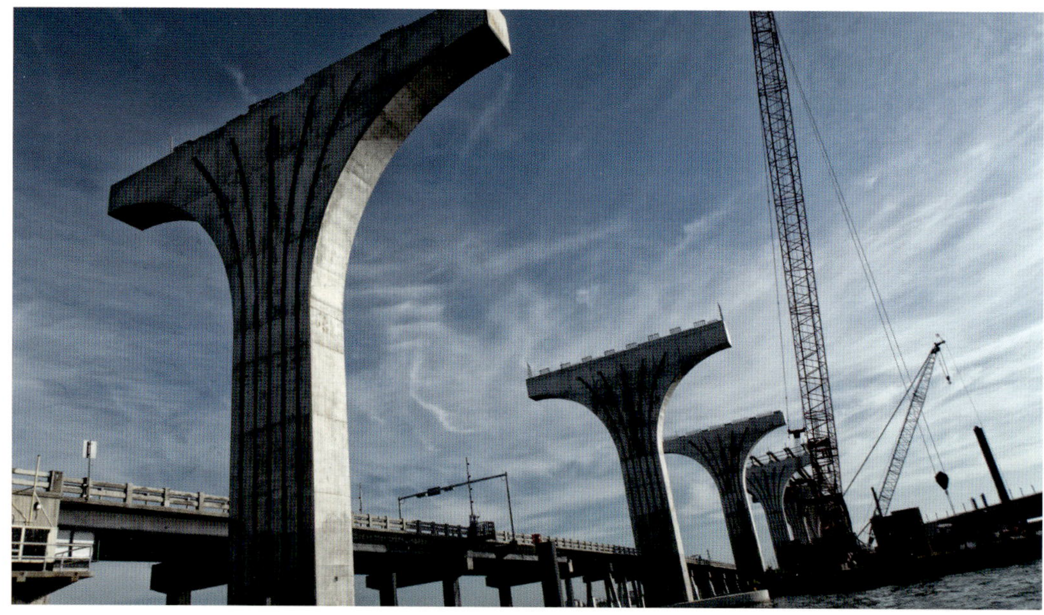

A new bridge replacing the old. The last century has seen a tremendous boom in construction throughout the state. A reflection of Florida's growing population, roads can disrupt the natural hydrology of the land, causing flooding in areas that rarely had a problem before, while simultaneously choking wetlands on lower ground.

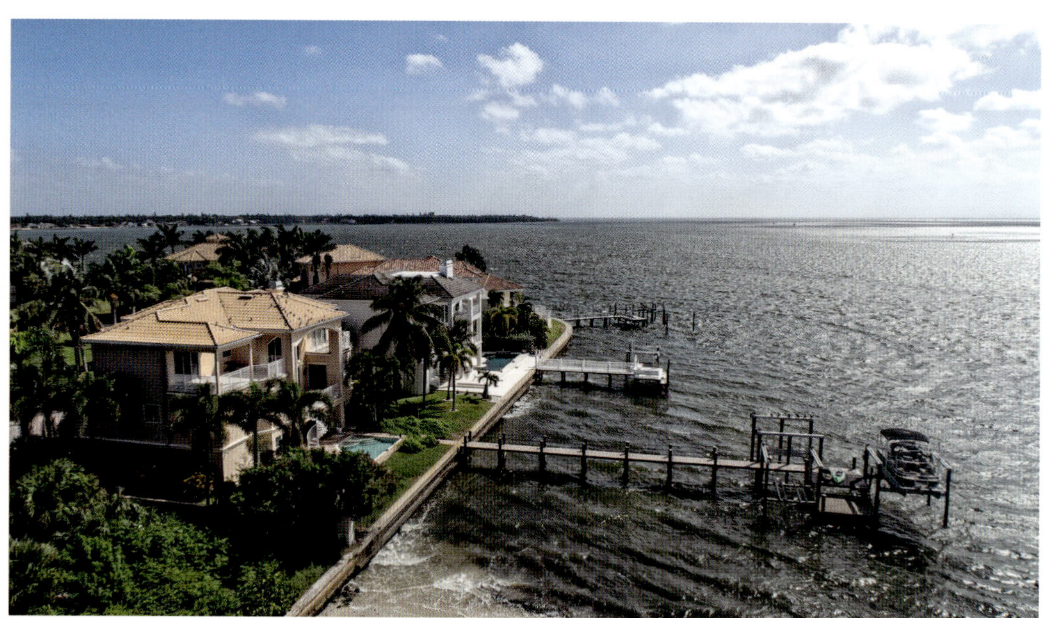

Facing the caprice of nature head-on—these homes on Florida's Gulf Coast stand on the site of a former mangrove forest. They enjoy a great view of the water, but face almost certain destruction should a hurricane make landfall in the vicinity.

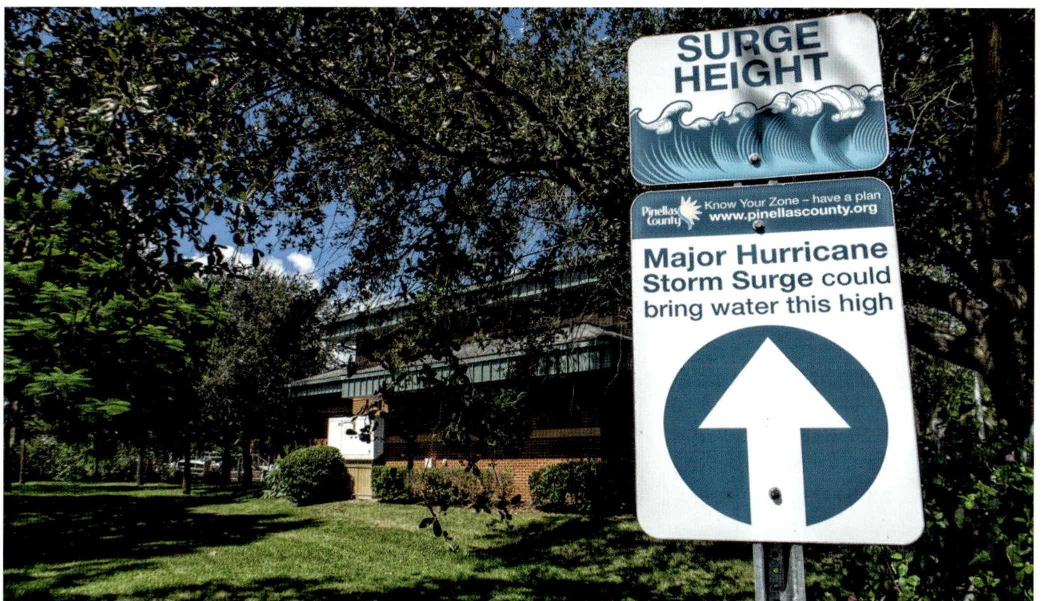

A warning sign on the road ahead.

In 1968—in the wake of 1965's Hurricane Betsy, which wrought historic devastation across parts of Florida and Louisiana—Congress authorized the National Flood Insurance Program, creating a federally-subsidized flood insurance market. This was a somewhat unprecedented act in terms of scale and scope, but in many ways, this massive intervention in the free market did not go far enough.

The consequence of this magnanimous federal act, whether intentional or not, is most clearly on display back here in Florida.

Coupled with the regular availability of disaster relief funds in the wake of major hurricanes, the federal government's flood insurance program dramatically reduces the financial risk of building in low-lying areas. Why not build big when large portions of flood repairs will be covered by the public?

Disaster relief is a basic responsibility of any functioning government—the definition of promoting the general welfare. But it is worth asking why the United States government continues to subsidize and incentivize unsustainable development along our coastlines, especially at a time when we increasingly understand the risks of climate change—not to mention the important role that restoring coastal wetlands such as mangroves might play in protecting human populations from its most acute effects.

What if, instead, the United States adopted a policy of encouraging a managed retreat—of buying out high-risk homes as they are destroyed rather than rebuilding them, then restoring the newly-public plot to its native ecosystem? No one should be forced to move, but the condition of financial relief at a catastrophic storm event comes with a slice of sound environmental policy.

As it turns out, the framework for such a seemingly radical plan exists. FEMA already has a perfunctory buyback program.

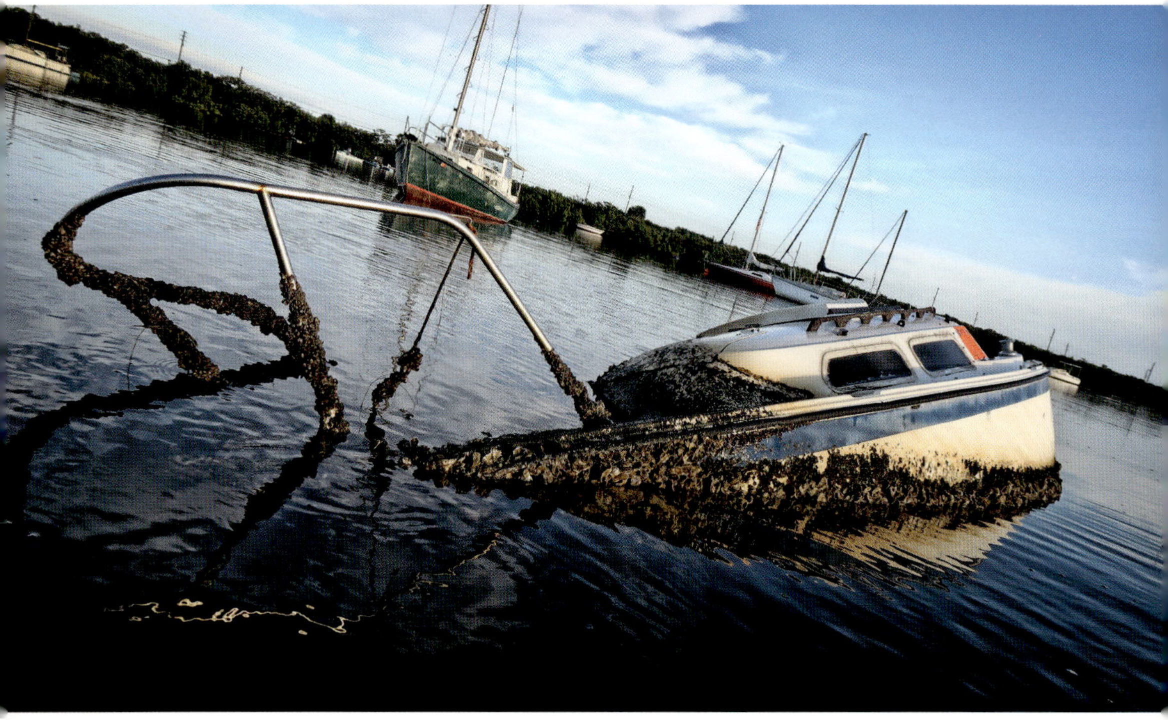

One of many derelict boats that wash up among the mangroves.

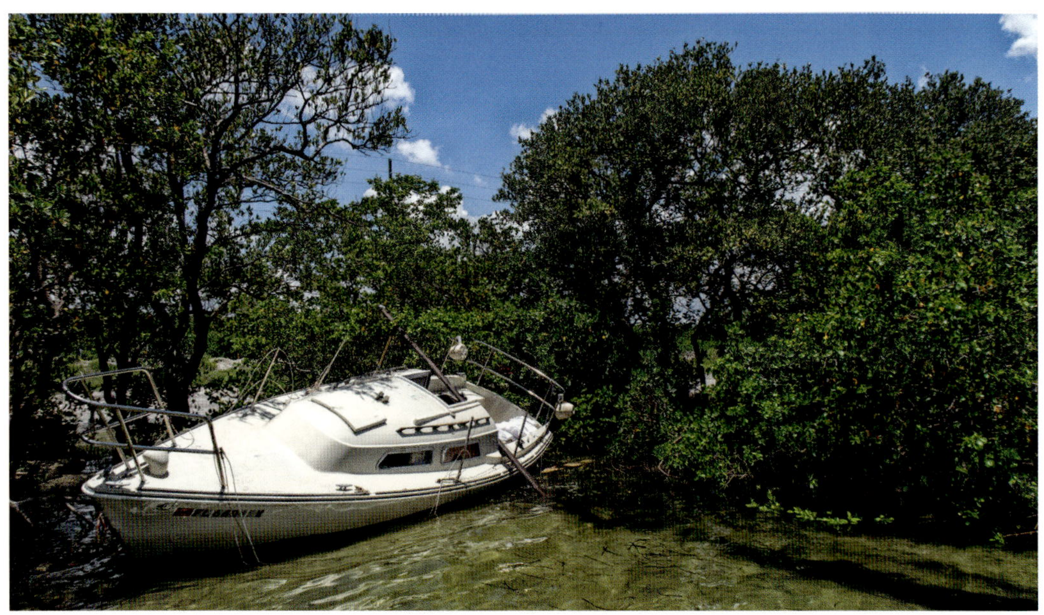

How many hopes and dreams are dashed, what tragic misfortunes are symbolized by an abandoned sailboat—that ultimate talisman of "the good life" gone south?

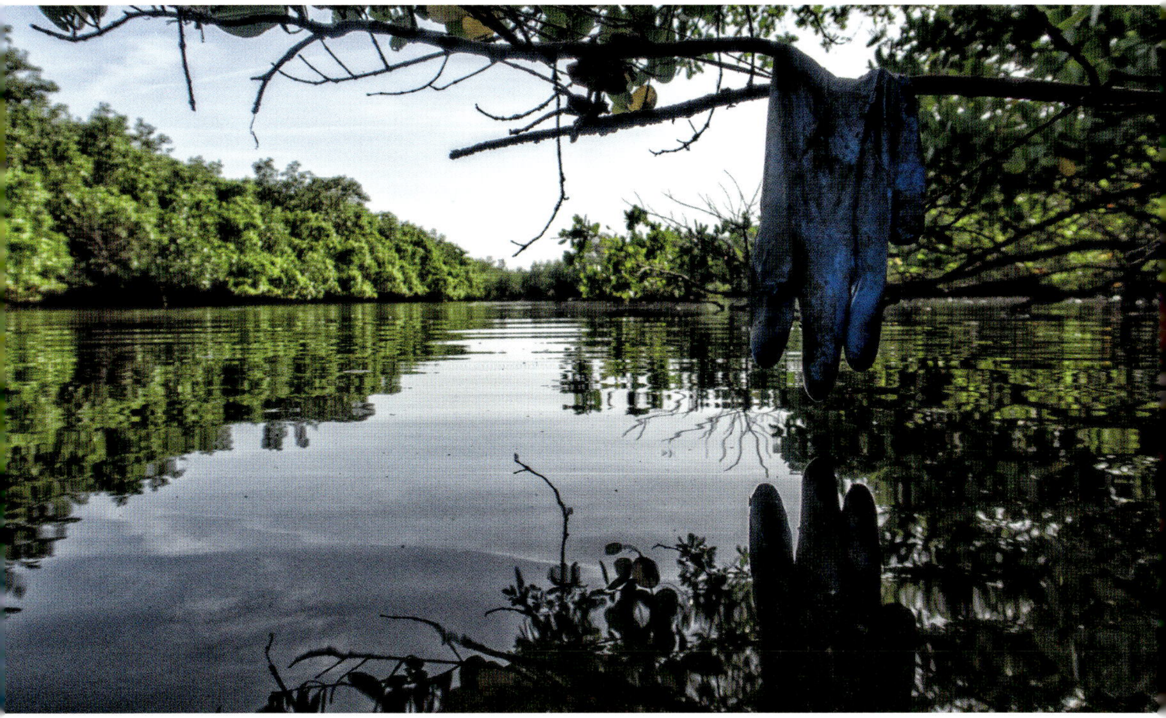

The hand of man is everywhere.

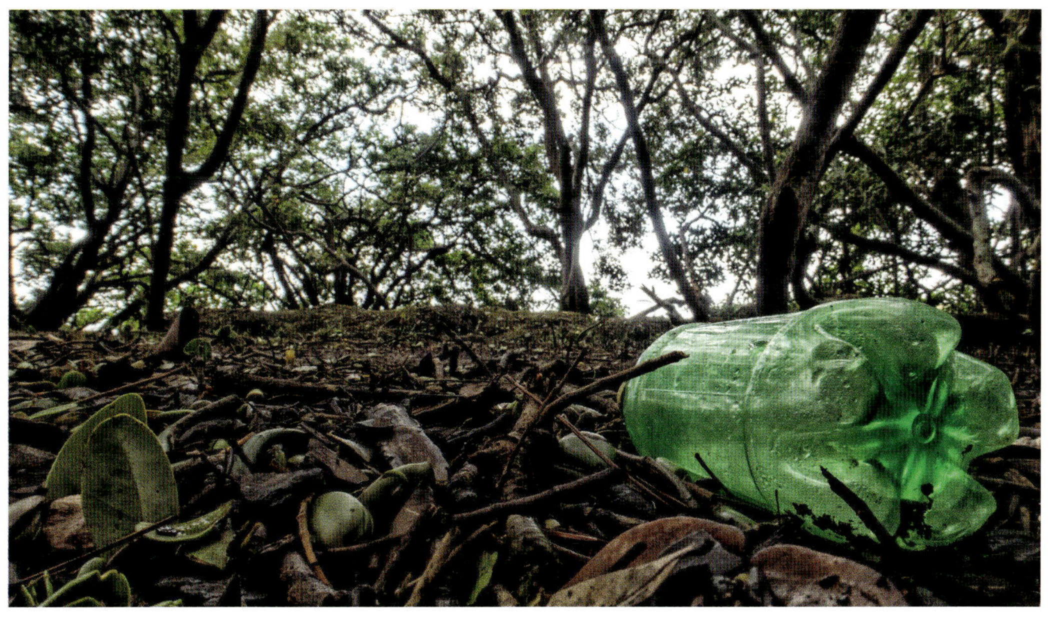

According to a 2017 piece in *The New York Times*, "The Natural Resources Defense Council estimates that the government has spent about $5.5 billion since 1978 to rebuild 30,000 homes that have flooded as many as five times in a two- or three-year period. The group estimates that buying many of these homes would cost less than the government spends in rebuilding them over and over. FEMA does finance buyouts but it spends vastly more to rebuild properties."[5]

On its website, FEMA explains its buyout program almost as if it is trying to talk you out of it:

> The decision to offer buyouts is made by the state using money that FEMA allocates through its Hazard Mitigation Grant Program to reduce future disaster losses. Seventy-five percent of any buyout cost is paid by FEMA and the rest is paid by the state and/or local government.
>
> It is not a simple process and requires agreement by your local government officials, the state and FEMA. It is important to note that many flooded properties don't qualify for a buyout, funding is limited and requests for funding may exceed available resources.
>
> Buyouts are voluntary and no one is required to sell their property.[6]

The government cannot stop bowling-ball hurricanes from barreling at Florida's long coastline, but it could stop resetting the pins frame after perverse frame.

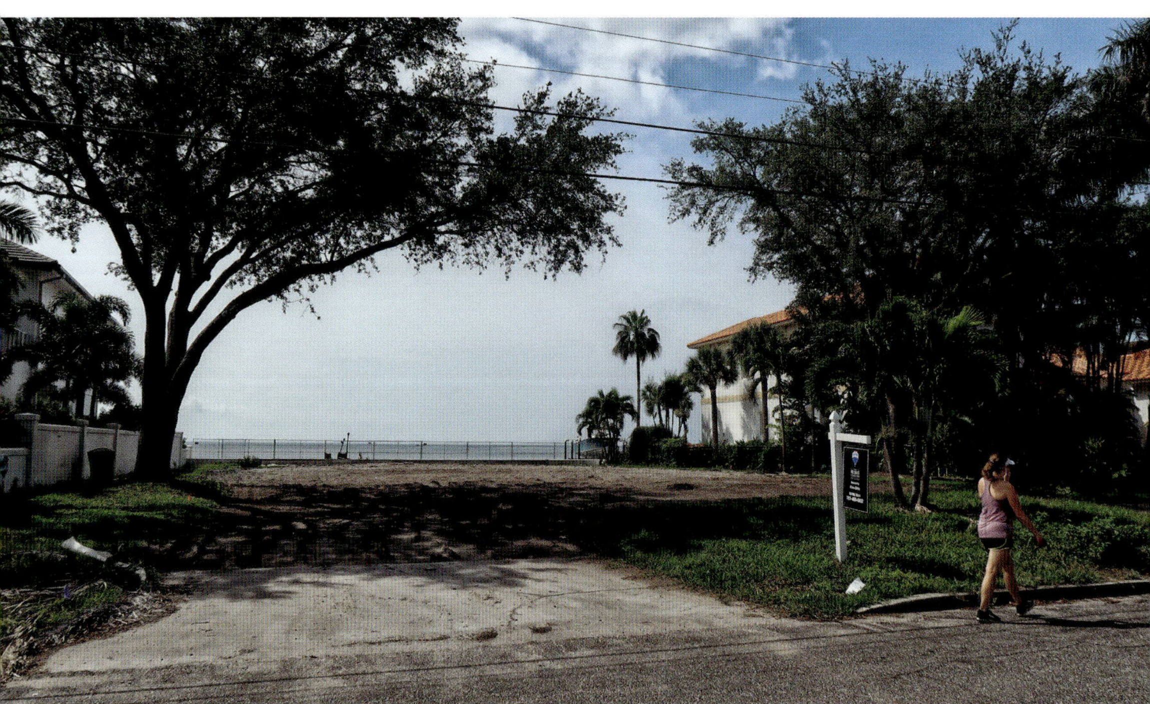

New listing. Is it responsible to rebuild on this low-lying land?

Perhaps the Floridians would be best served if we ate the admittedly steep cost of buying out the most vulnerable neighborhoods and restoring the wetlands upon which they were built. The relocation-conditional buyout should be made more financially attractive and attainable—the norm, rather than the exception in areas of high risk.

None of this—the buyouts, the restoration of wetlands—is as far-fetched as it seems. It is known as managed retreat, and despite the federal government's slow adoption of the concept, versions of it are already in practice on a local scale in flood prone areas throughout the nation. Given the staggering estimates for the cost of climate change if we do nothing to stem the tide in the present day—10.5 percent of the United States' GDP annually by the end of the twenty-first century, a substantial portion of that related to sea level rise and more severe hurricane impacts—some proactive investment in this department now would seem to be in order.[7]

I know this kind of solution will not be popular with everyone. But it does get to a central question about what we need from our elected officials—is it their job to do what is popular, or is it their mandate to do what is necessary? Theirs to do what is easy, or what is right?

In the grand scheme of things, Floridians would be better protected against the next storm if we ceded some substantial portion of our coastline land back to its rightful occupants—Mangrove National Monument, anyone?

Or, we can wait it out and hope against all available evidence that it's the storms and the seas that bend to our unwillingness to accept change.

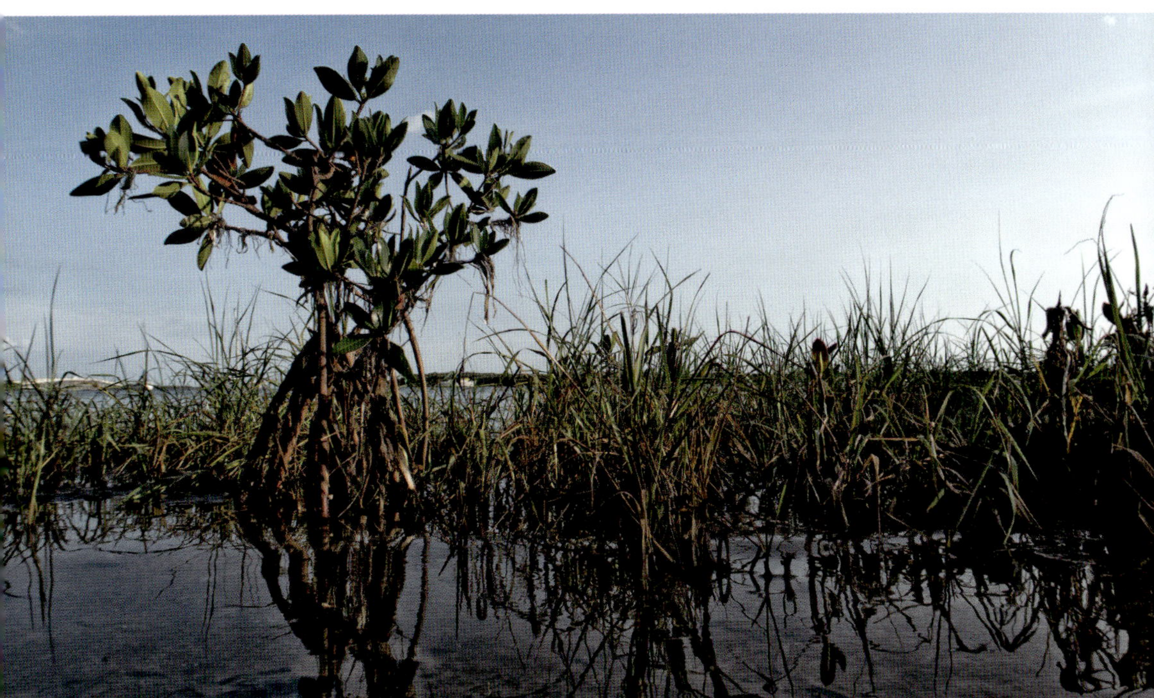

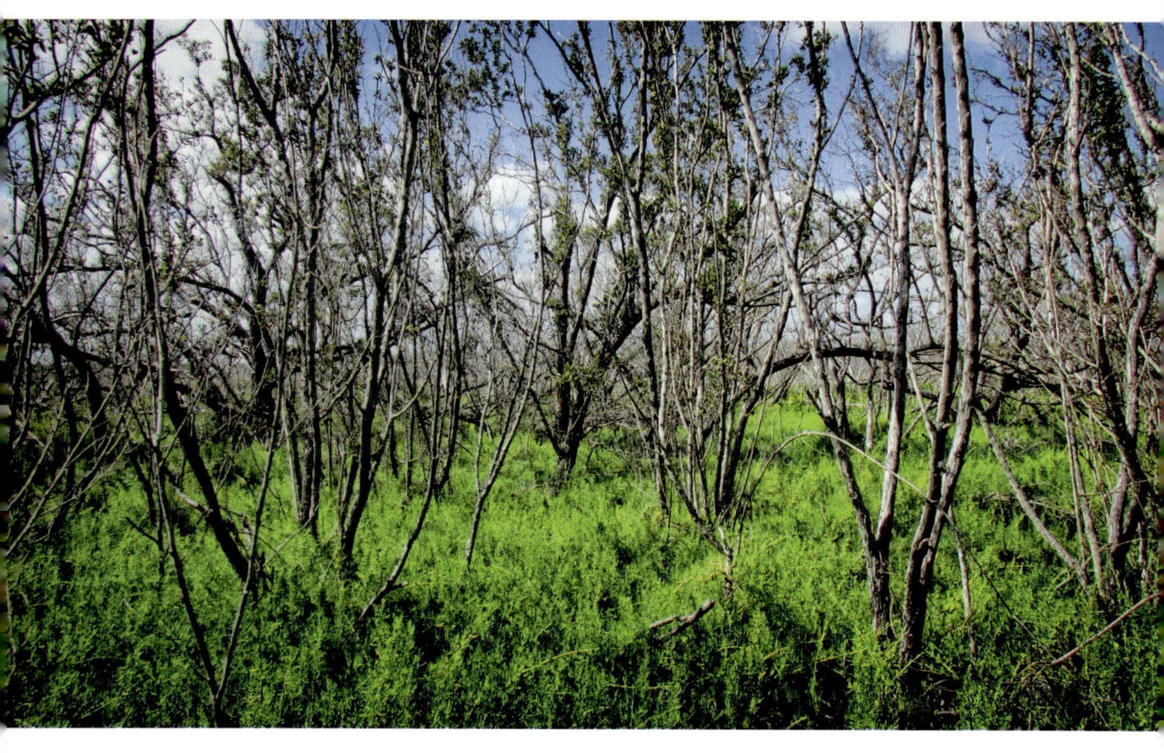

4

SORT OF SEMI-PROTECTED STATUS

*Natural mangrove ecosystems do not require management other than being left
alone. Mature mangrove systems are self-renewing and respond to perturbations
of the natural cycles of freeze, flood, and storm without the need for significant
human intervention. Unfortunately, in South Florida, most mangrove systems have
been degraded by human impacts either directly, as in spoil pile deposition or
impoundment, or indirectly by alteration of basin hydrology, as in Florida Bay and
the Everglades. Most management efforts require the removal of past effects as well
as the prevention of continued or future human impacts.*

"Mangroves: Multi-Species Recovery Plan for South Florida"
Report by the Federal Fish and Wildlife Service.[1]

Maligned with the name swamp, drained to combat mosquitoes, bulldozed for waterfront housing—the last century has not been kind to the humble mangrove.

No one seems to have a handle on exactly how many acres of mangrove forest have been lost to human activity over the last century because—frankly—until fairly recently, no one was even trying to keep track. A 1985 paper estimated a 23-percent loss since the 1940s.[2] The same paper claimed 674,241 acres of extant mangrove forest in that middle year of the 1980s. A quarter of the way through the twenty-first century, official estimates say that Florida's mangrove coverage has fallen to 469,000—a loss of 200,000 acres since the 1980s. Almost all of what remains is within local, state, and national parkland, or preserved for the time being on auxiliary land surrounding power plants, ports, and industrial plants.

If case studies on specific regions such as Tampa Bay, Indian River, or the Lake Worth regions are representative—conducted via methods such as the comparison of modern satellite imagery with aerial photos of mangrove swamps taken in the 1940s—the state may have lost, impounded, or otherwise impaired between 40 and 86 percent of its mangrove forests during the twentieth century.[3]

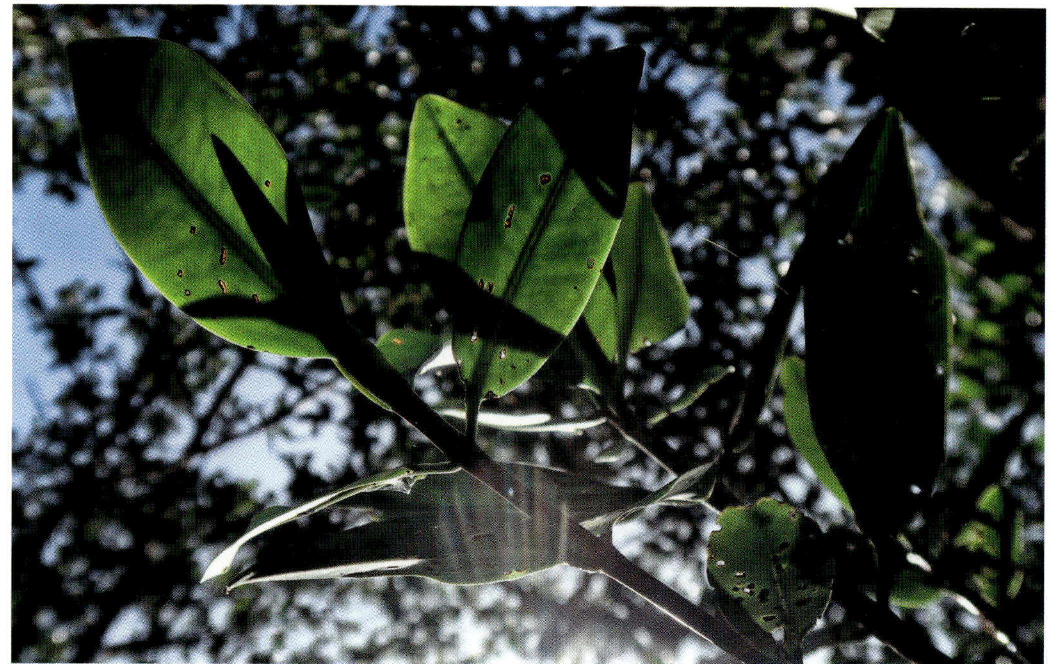

A ray of sunshine.

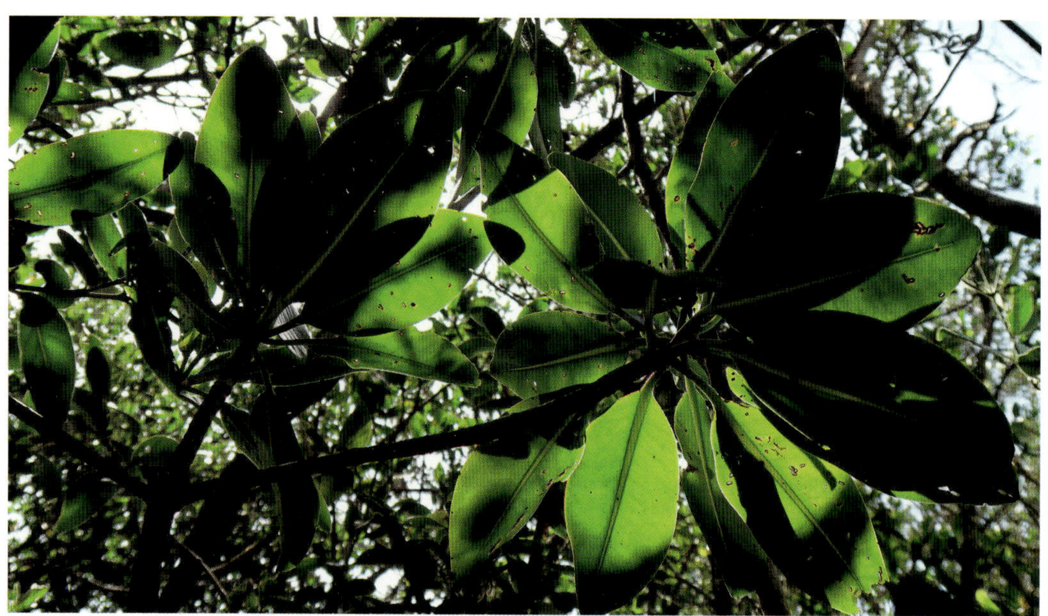

Everglades National Park contains the largest contiguous stretch of protected mangrove forest in the western hemisphere.

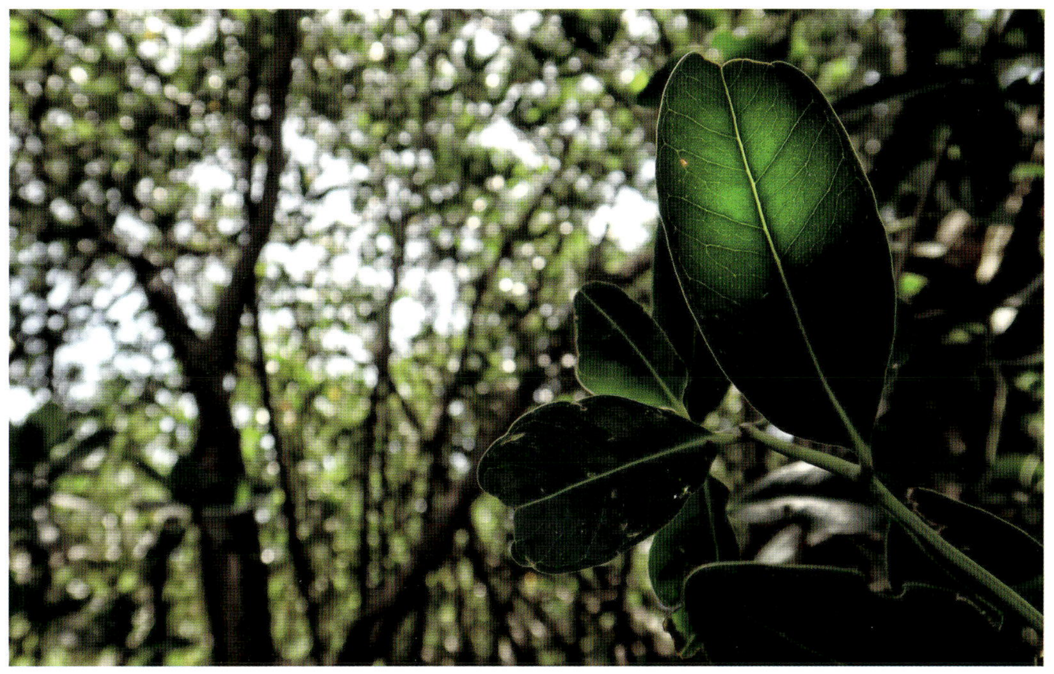

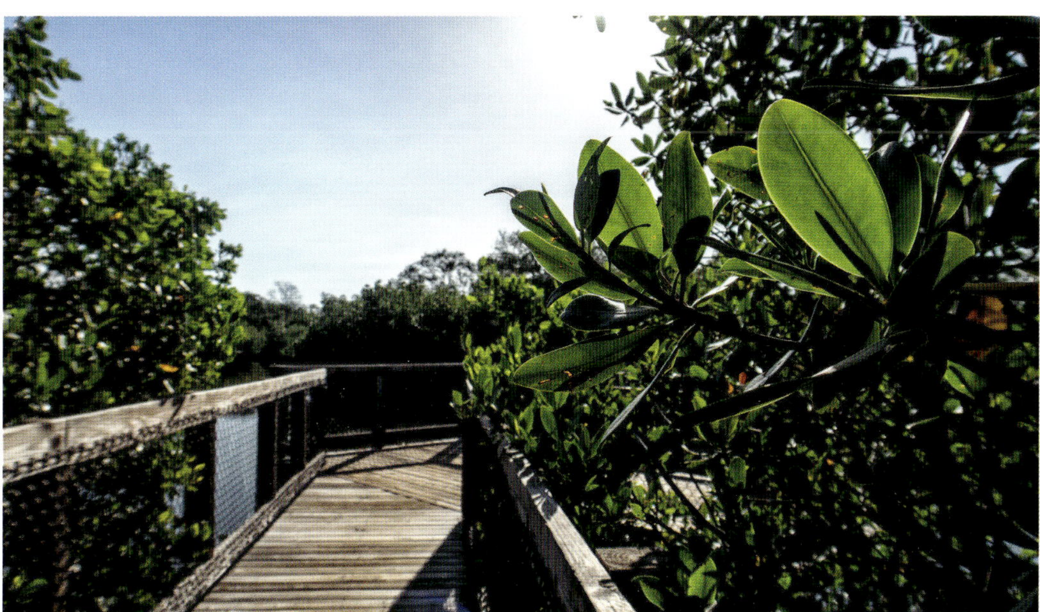

Clam Bayou represents a success for mangroves. The Southwest Florida Water Management District assumed management of this estuary in cooperation with the cities of Gulfport and St. Petersburg. Prior to 1995, it was a heavily-polluted space—silted up, full of litter, and prone to algal blooms. More deliberate wastewater management and careful dredging has restored natural tidal flushing and transformed Clam Bayou into a thriving mangrove forest.

Extensive protected stands of mangrove forest in remote sections of Everglades National Park might mean that numbers from those higher, more catastrophic case studies—conducted in areas with high rates of population growth in the twentieth century—cannot be extrapolated to the state as a whole. But based on the 1985 estimate and these more localized case studies, a 40-percent loss since the *de facto* baseline count in the 1940s seems plausible, and maybe even conservative. This would represent the destruction and disruption of nearly half a million acres of mangrove forest.

There is just so much we just do not know—beginning with just how much we have lost!

Mangroves enjoy only weak federal protection outside of national parks. Some creatures on the Endangered Species List—such as the wood stork (*Mycteria americana*)—make their home in mangroves, extending at least a flimsy umbrella of protection over the whole habitat.

The Clean Water Act of 1972 is also supposed to offer a degree of protection to certain mangrove forests, requiring environmental impact assessments of any development that might impact nearby wetlands. In practice, these laws are often in tension with market forces. Plenty of industry groups whose interests compete with conservation have in recent years prevailed upon the federal government to reduce oversight of wetlands.

In 2020, this push culminated in the EPA ceding its power under the Clean Water Act to approve or reject projects impacting Florida's wetlands. This arrangement makes Florida one of only three states with such unencumbered authority. The governor celebrated the fact that this will bring regulation closer to home, which, in turn, is exactly what critics of the decision are afraid of.

Even before this devolution of authority was finalized, the National Oceanic and Atmospheric Administration, charged with "fisheries management, coastal restoration and supporting marine commerce"—characterized the status of mangroves in decidedly fatalistic terms. "Mangrove habitat in the Florida Keys has been destroyed largely by urbanization of the Keys from the late 1950s through the 1980s. The large-scale loss of mangroves has all but ceased … due to laws protecting wetlands; however, these laws are continuously under threat of being relaxed."[4] Though in this passage, NOAS was writing specifically about the Keys, they could just as well have been talking about the state of Florida as a whole.

The mangrove enjoys some degree of protected status under Florida state law.

Under the Mangrove Trimming and Preservation Act of 1996, the state's first and so far only major legislative attempt at protecting its dwindling mangrove forests, property owners may trim or alter mangroves to improve views of the water or to allow for access to navigable waterways.[5]

If a mangrove on private land is over 6 feet tall but under 10, the landowner may prune mangroves themselves—outside of those specifications, they must hire a licensed professional, who often requires a state permit specific to that trimming job. If an owner wishes to remove a mangrove entirely, they may do so, but must plant two of the same species elsewhere on the same property.

Fines are issued for violations—ranging between $420 and $10,000, according to a report by *USA Today*.[6]

It seems that this law, under a best-case scenario, will maintain the diminished *status quo*—which is no small thing, considering what came before.

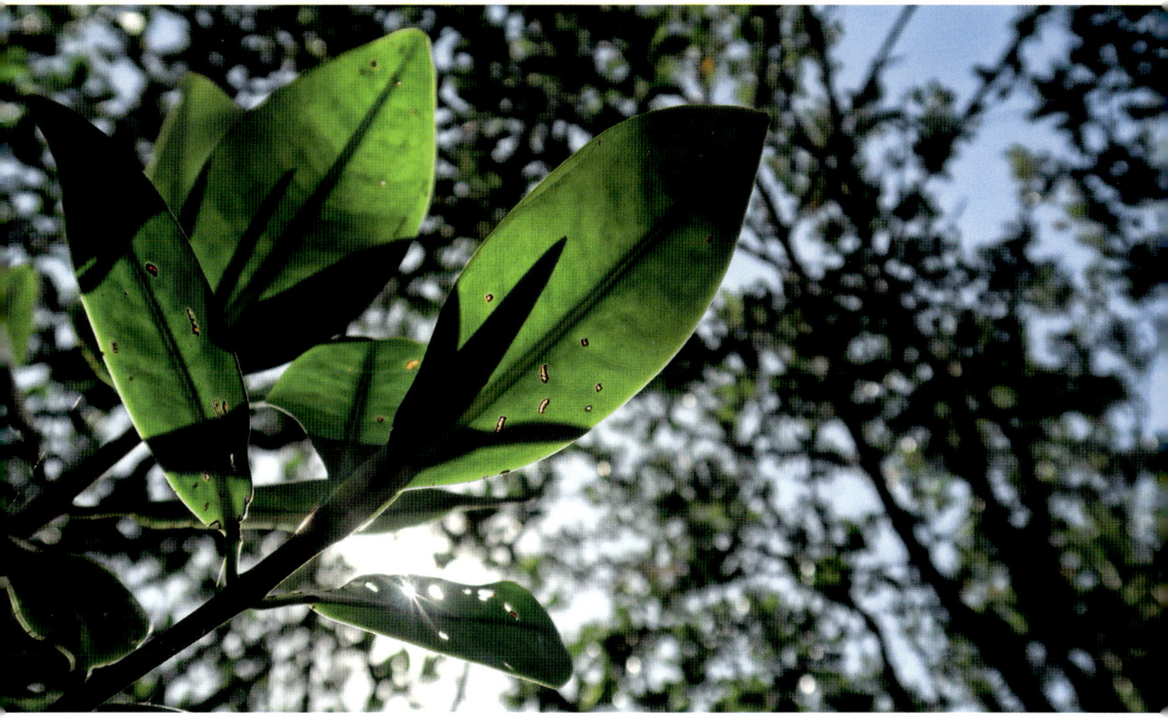

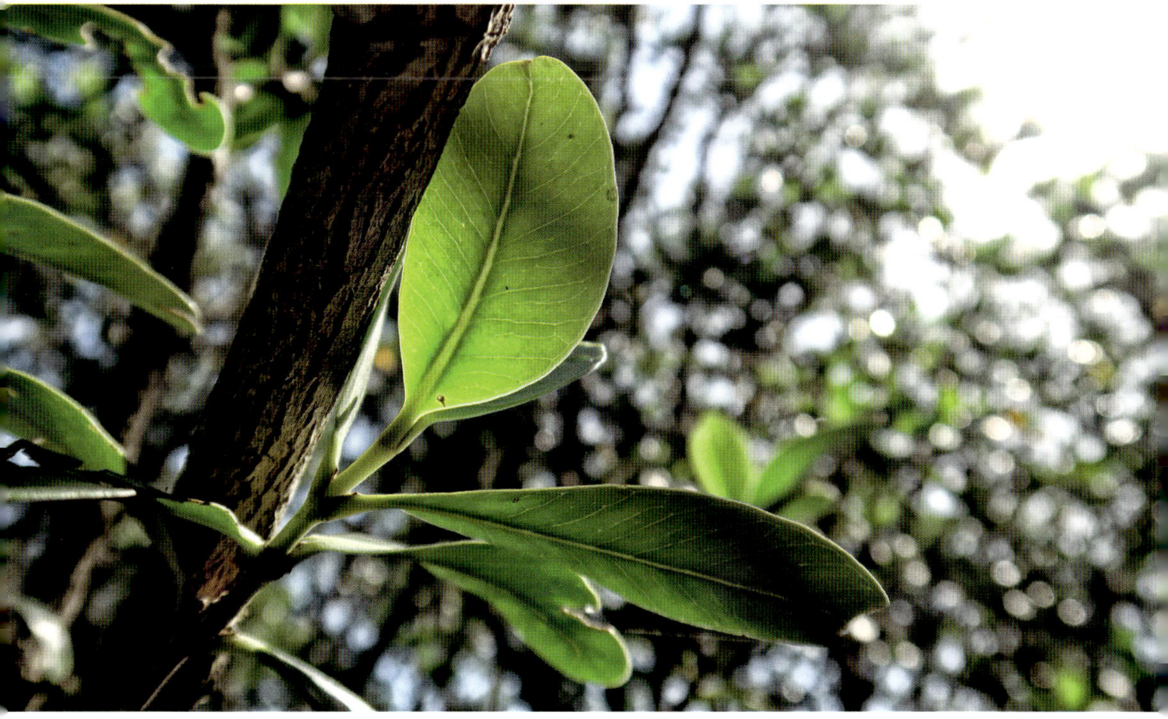

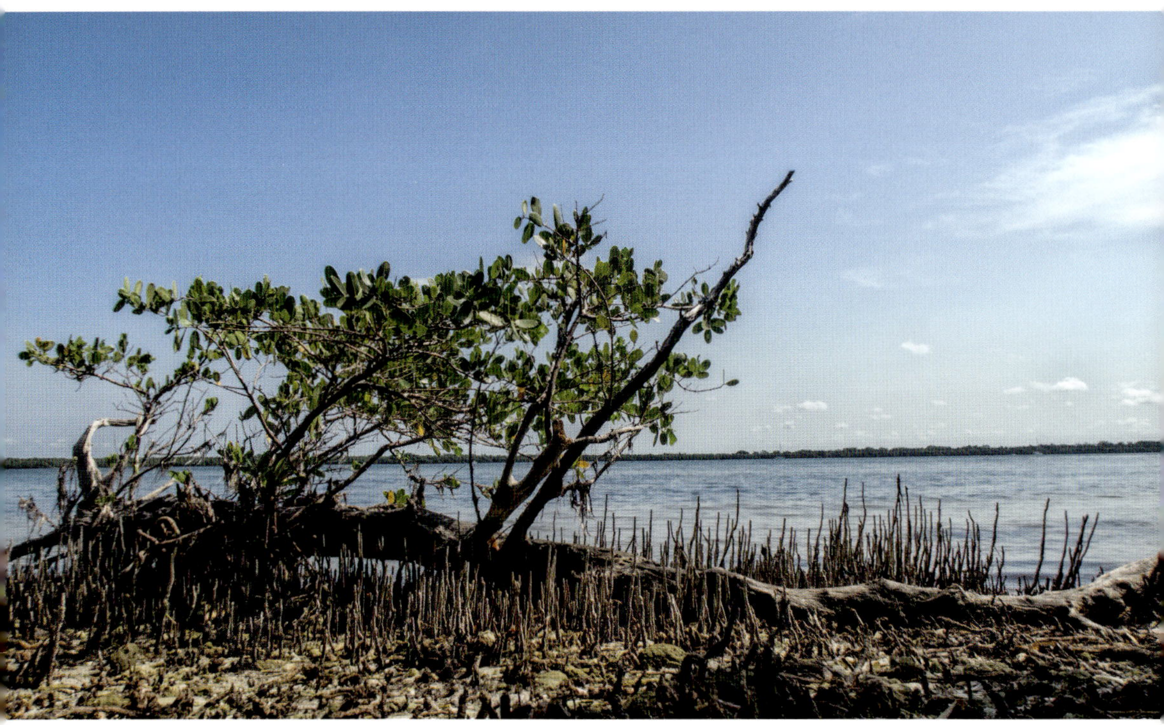

What else might be done?

It is conceivable that governments might go a step further, offering tax incentives to homeowners who allowed mangroves to flourish on their properties—a sort of homestead exemption for the original occupants of the lands. However, unless Florida's conservative legislature adopts a sudden conservationist bent, such a policy is probably even less likely than an expansion of post-disaster buyouts at the federal level.

As is par for the course under many of Florida's environmental regulations—which govern everything from single use plastics to waterfront development—no local jurisdiction is allowed to impose more restrictive rules than those adopted by the state. This doctrine of preemption means that unless those in Tallahassee or Washington reevaluate their priorities, more energetic conservation or restoration projects outside of established parklands will mostly be philanthropic, borne of goodwill by individuals and nonprofits—or carried out as isolated penance for specific environmental disasters.

One case of the latter is a $5 million mangrove restoration project undertaken by fertilizer giant Mosaic Company along the Alafia River—a waterway that, like so many, has been straightened, dredged, contained, and otherwise transformed to better meet the needs of industry over the course of the twentieth century.

In 2004, a breach in one of Mosaic's gypsum storage stacks spewed millions of gallons of acidic wastewater into Tampa Bay, poisoning any fish or mangrove unfortunate enough to be in the vicinity at the time. After an investigation by relevant authorities, the company agreed to mitigate the environmental consequences of this disaster through projects on nearby company-held lands.[7]

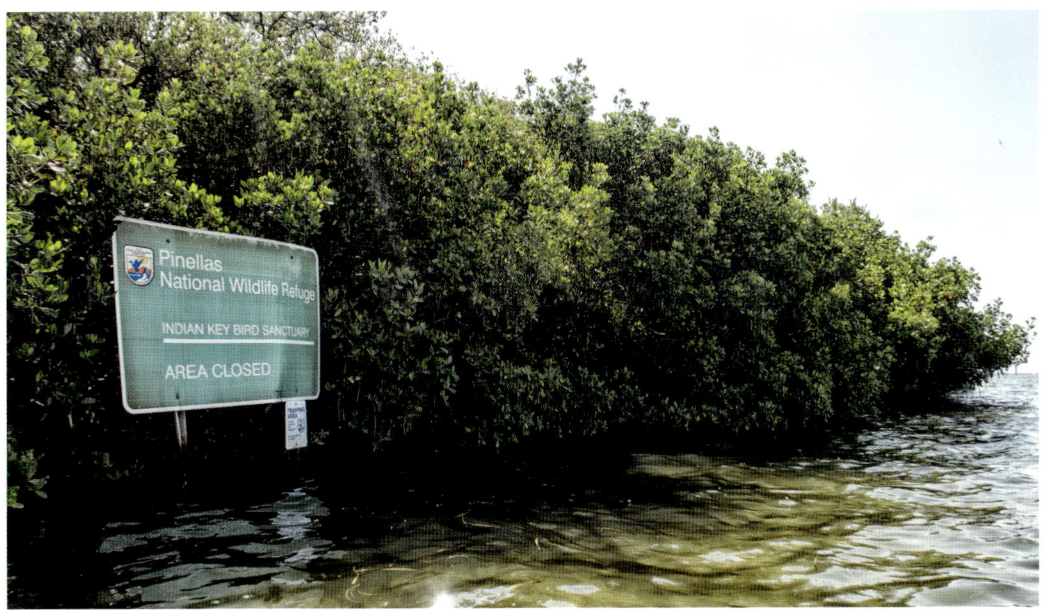

Many mangroves lie within wildlife sanctuaries, protected by virtue of their role as an important nesting habitat for birds.

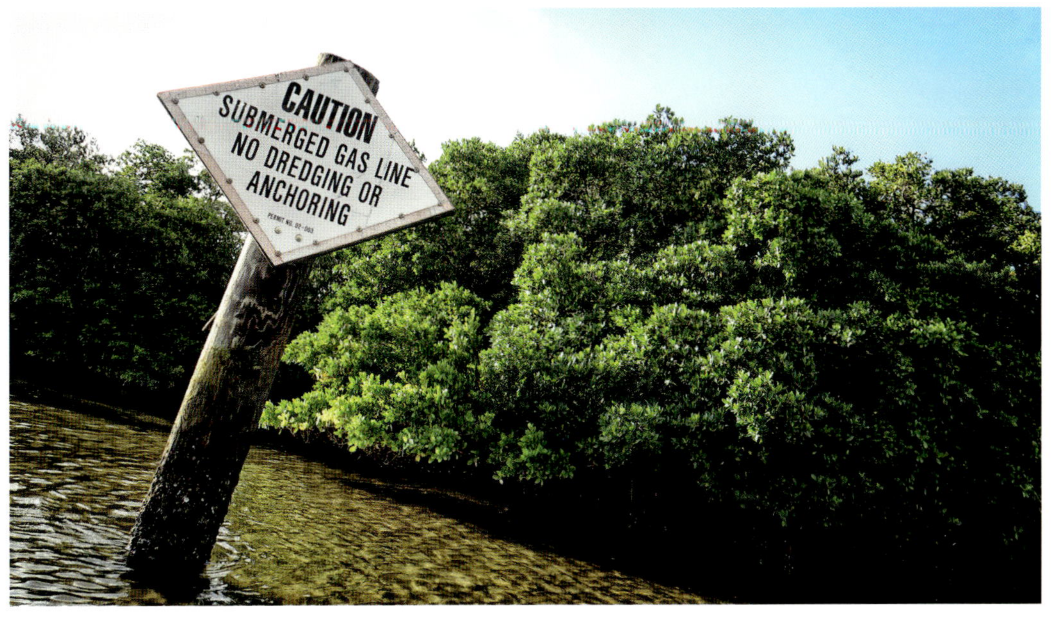

Other mangrove forests are protected by their proximity to power plants and other industrial centers, situated near the shore to accommodate their appetite for a steady source of water.

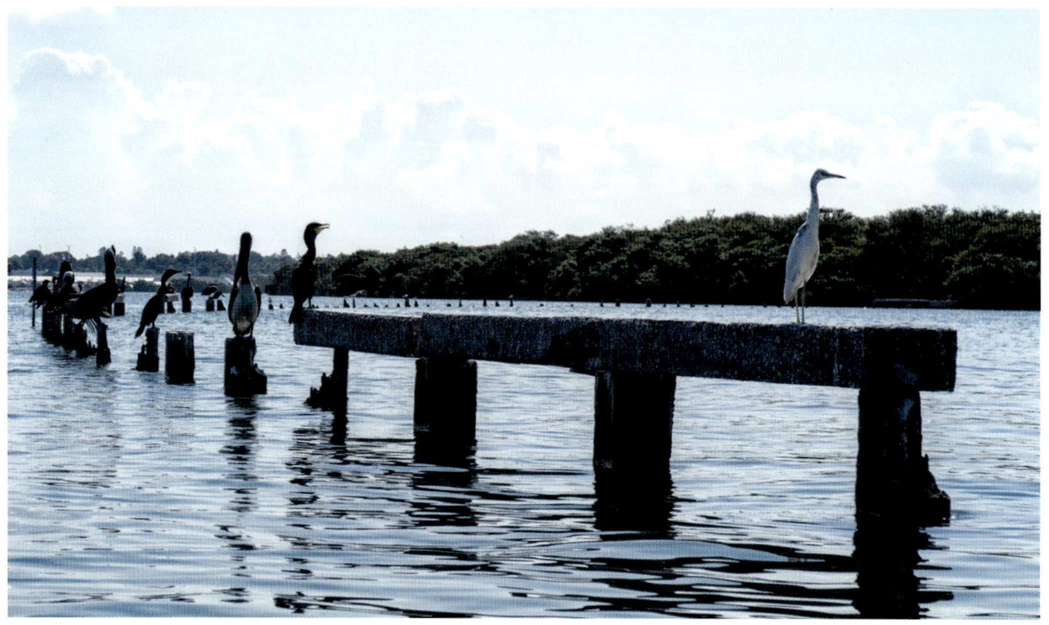

A bird sanctuary, out of bounds to anyone who doesn't make their home amongst the mangroves. What is wild about a space like this is how little we can trust our own species to tread lightly.

Working in consultation with the Environmental Protection Commission of Hillsborough County, the Florida Department of Environmental Protection, and the National Oceanic and Atmospheric Administration, Mosaic opened up a 50-foot-wide channel in a breakwater, mimicking the Alafia River's historic flow through some 85 acres of mangroves.

The project is still new, in the grand scheme of things—but the early results are promising. Mangroves and all of the species that depend upon them are experiencing a revival in the mitigation area, which had previously been in pretty sorry shape after decades of restriction. That is a win.

It should not be surprising to anyone paying attention just how easily nature reasserts itself when man gets out of the way.

And 85 additional acres of healthy mangrove habitat is something! But, in comparison to all that has been lost, the Alafia River project seems like such a token down payment to the Earth.

It throws into striking contrast our startling "normal."

Maintaining the well-being of mangroves on company land is seen as a punishment, rather than as par for the course—rather than the sane, sustainable cost of doing business in the state of Florida. It is a shame that only under the extreme circumstances of an industrial accident do we expect anything approaching stewardship from the businesses that extract so much wealth from our natural world.

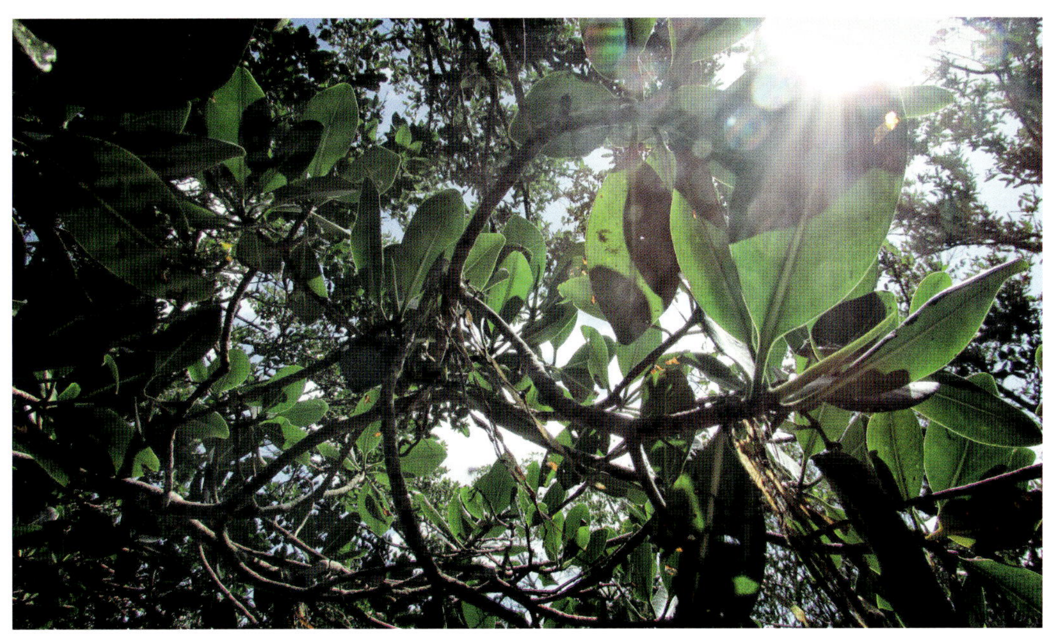

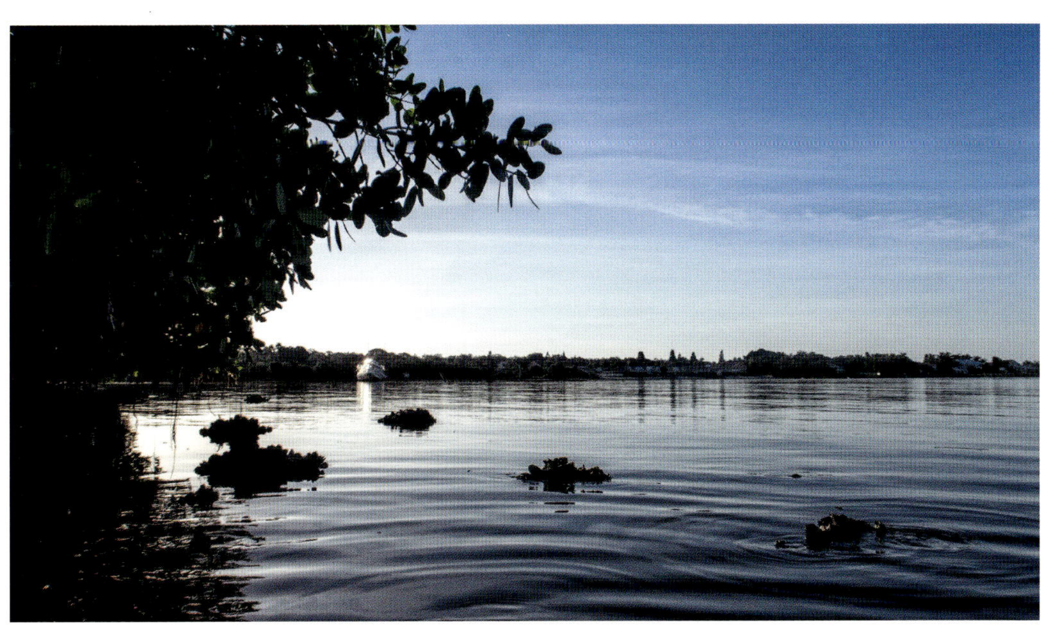

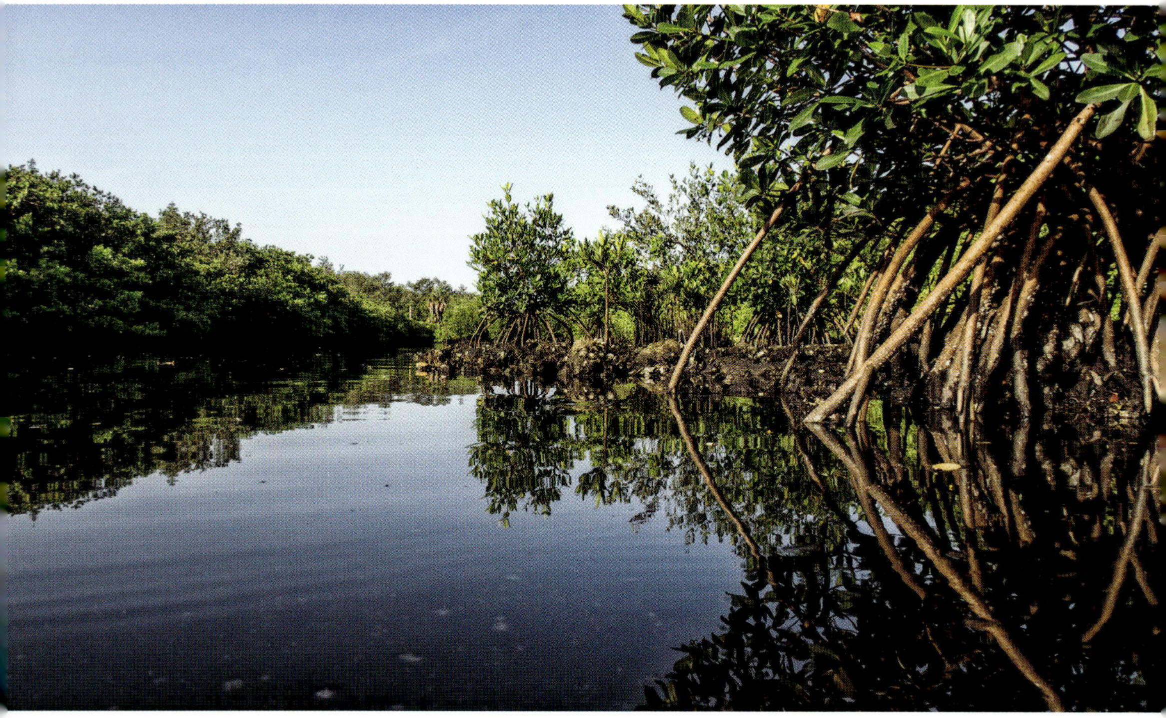

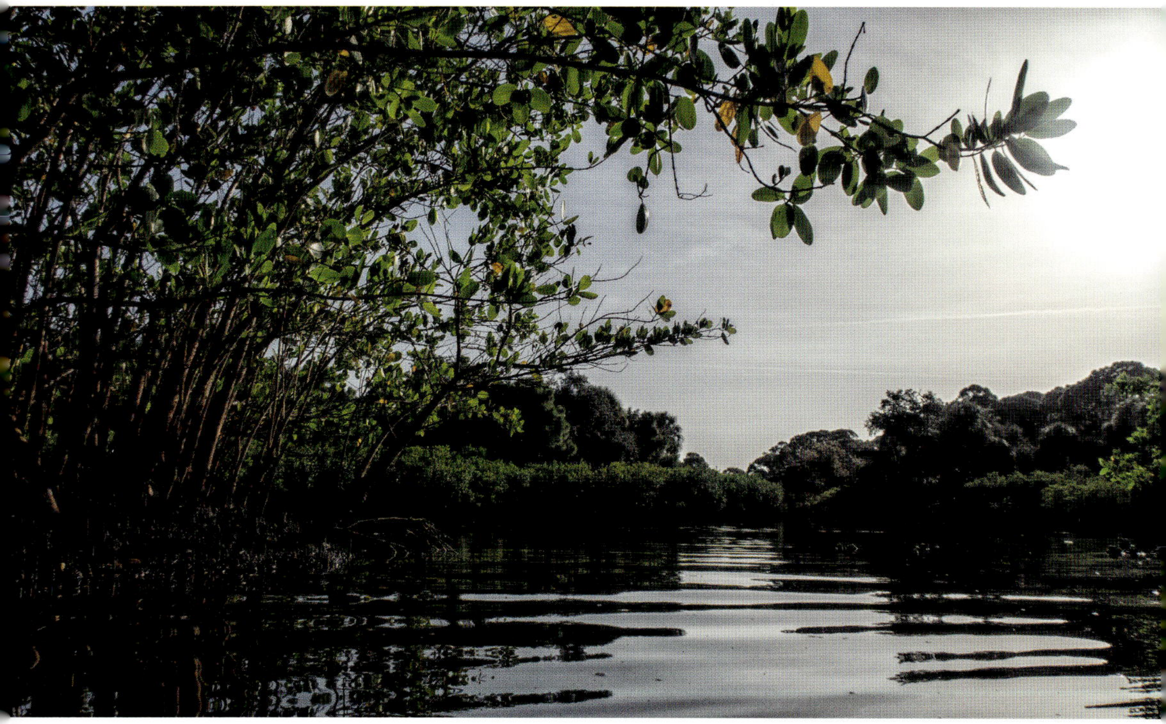

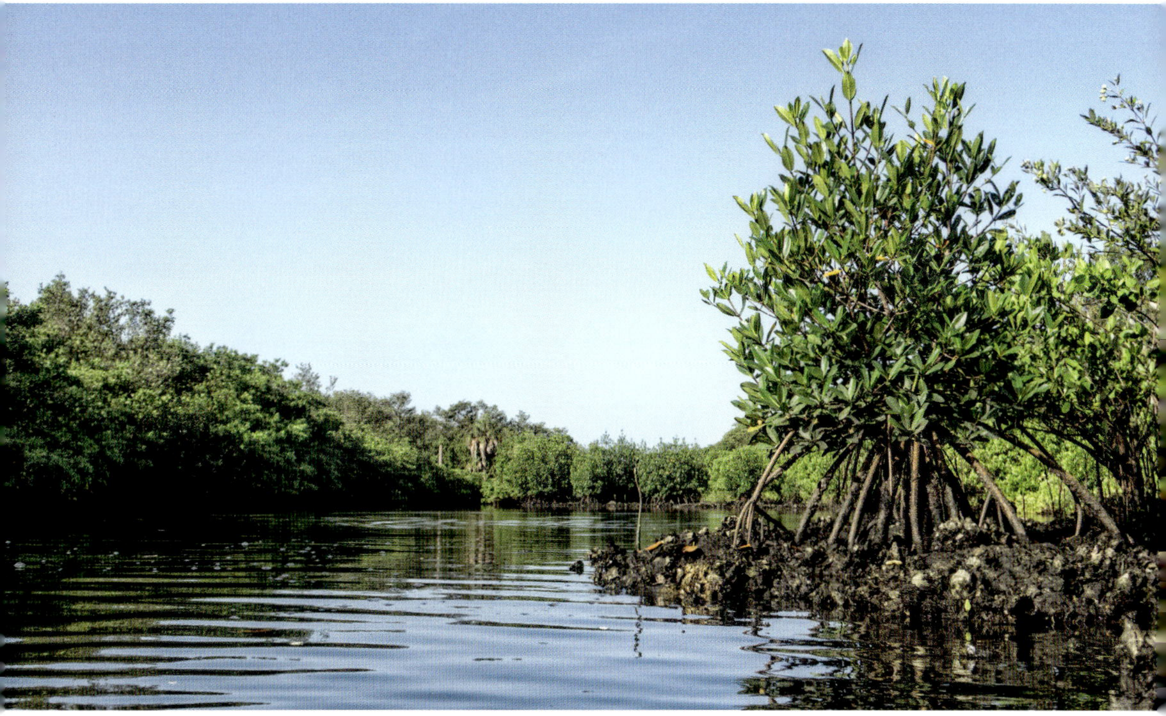

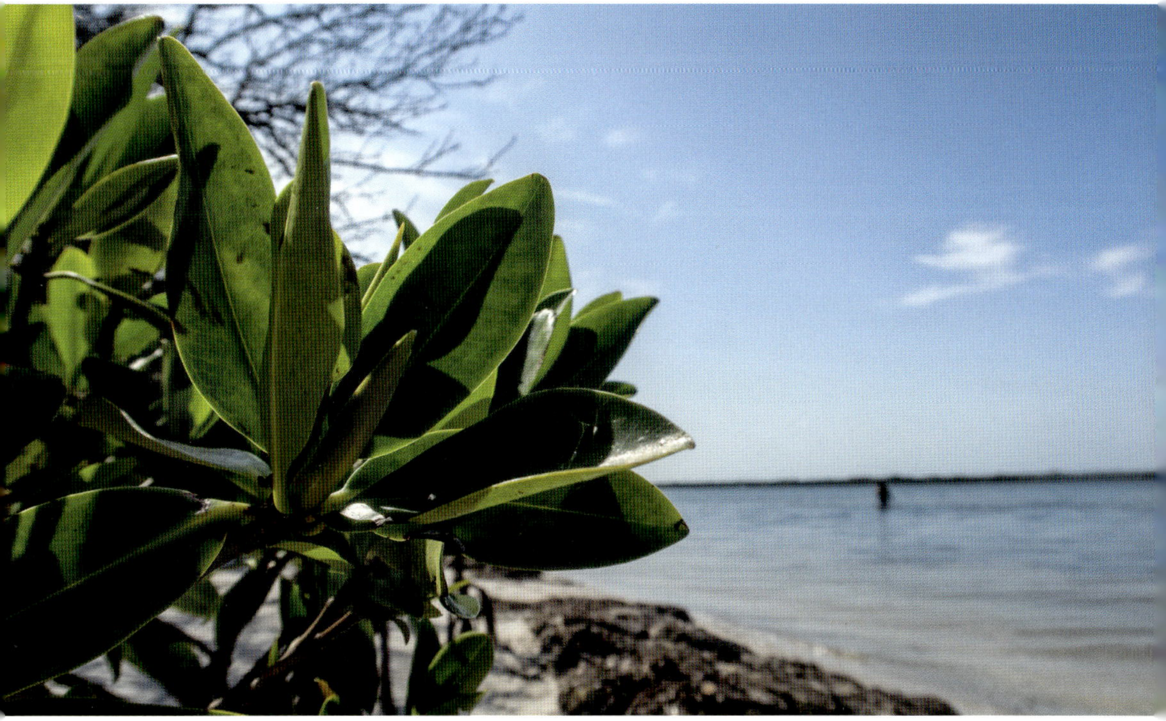

5

DOOM OR SALVATION IN CLIMATE CHANGE

Everybody needs beauty as well as bread, places to play in and pray in, where nature may heal and give strength to body and soul alike.

John Muir

Some 20,000 years ago, at the height of the last ice age, Florida's mangroves stood along the peninsula's prehistoric coastline, at least a 100 miles west of modern Tampa Bay. Over the intervening millennia, the predecessors of today's mangrove forests have crept in and out to accommodate Florida's shifting intertidal zone, scrambling like late afternoon beachgoers moving their towels as the tide rushes in.[1]

And the tide, so to speak, is rushing in—the question is not "Will sea levels rise dramatically this century?" Rather, it is "Just how dramatically will sea levels rise—and how soon?"

Current sea level rise is equal to approximately 3.5 millimeters a year and accelerating. Mangroves seem to be coping for now, trapping sediment and forming their own elevated land at a similar pace. But researchers believe that a rate of sea level rise somewhere around 7 millimeters of year would pose a catastrophic threat to mangroves—a rate expected before the middle of this century.[2]

Given space to migrate, Florida's mangroves could do so, thriving more or less forever on the blurriest edges of our redrawn coastlines, just as they have for thousands of years. The problem this time around is that as sea levels rise, mangroves are finding themselves backed up against human industry and homes, arrayed just above the current high tide line all along the state's coast. As Florida adds something like a thousand new residents a day to its already considerable population—mangroves have little higher ground available for retreat.

Experts call this disastrous situation "coastal squeeze."[3]

And so, in many places, rising sea levels will lead to the complete inundation of mangrove props by saltwater, effectively suffocating the trees and extinguishing the rich biomes they support.

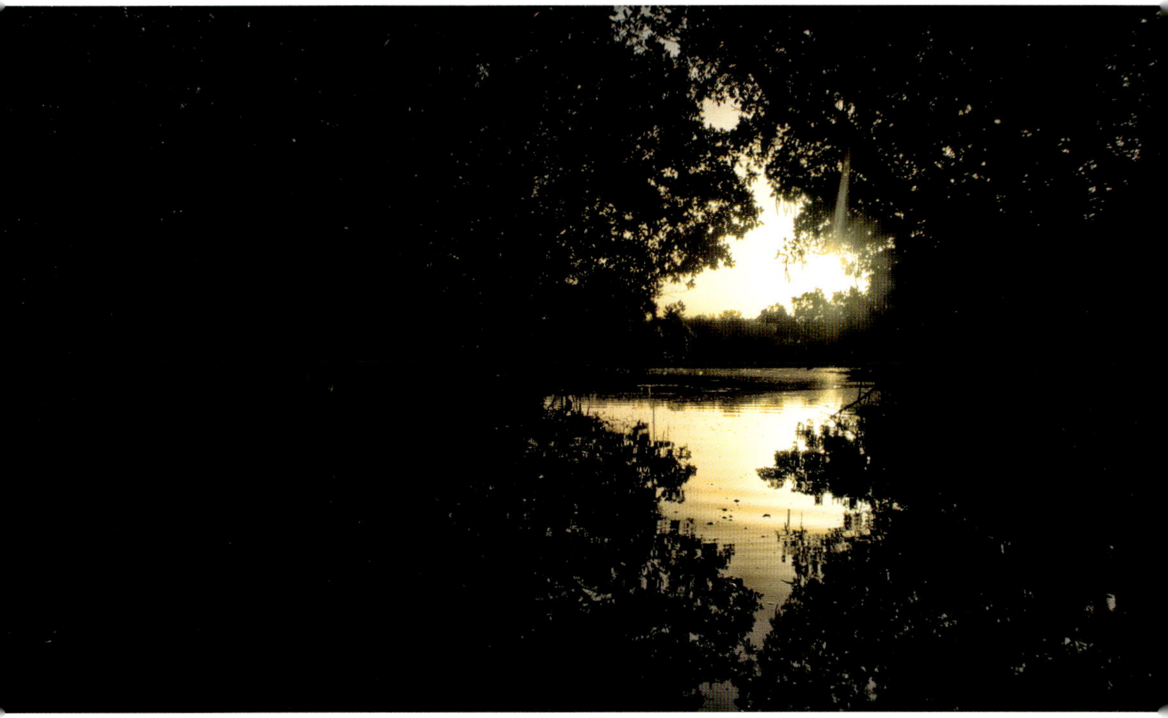

By dawn's early light.

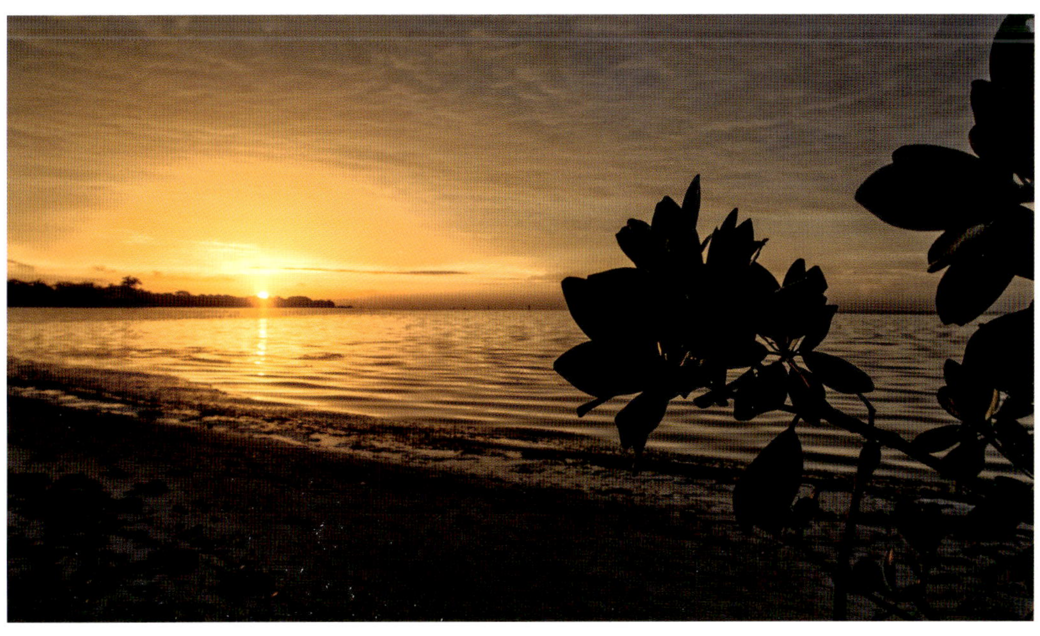

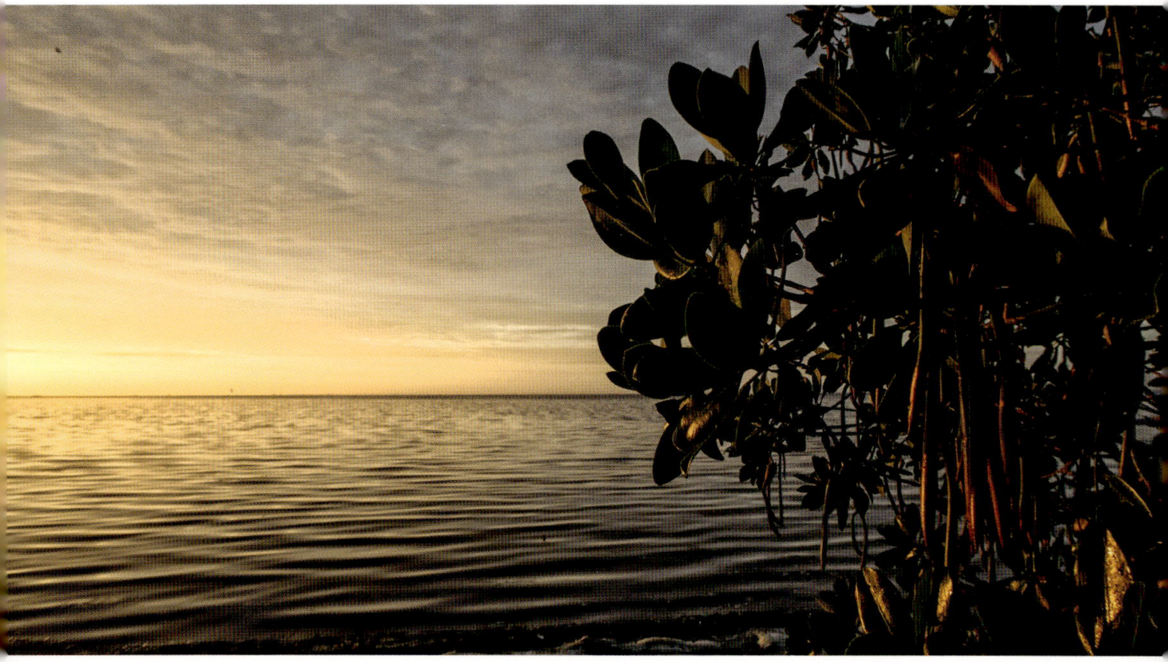

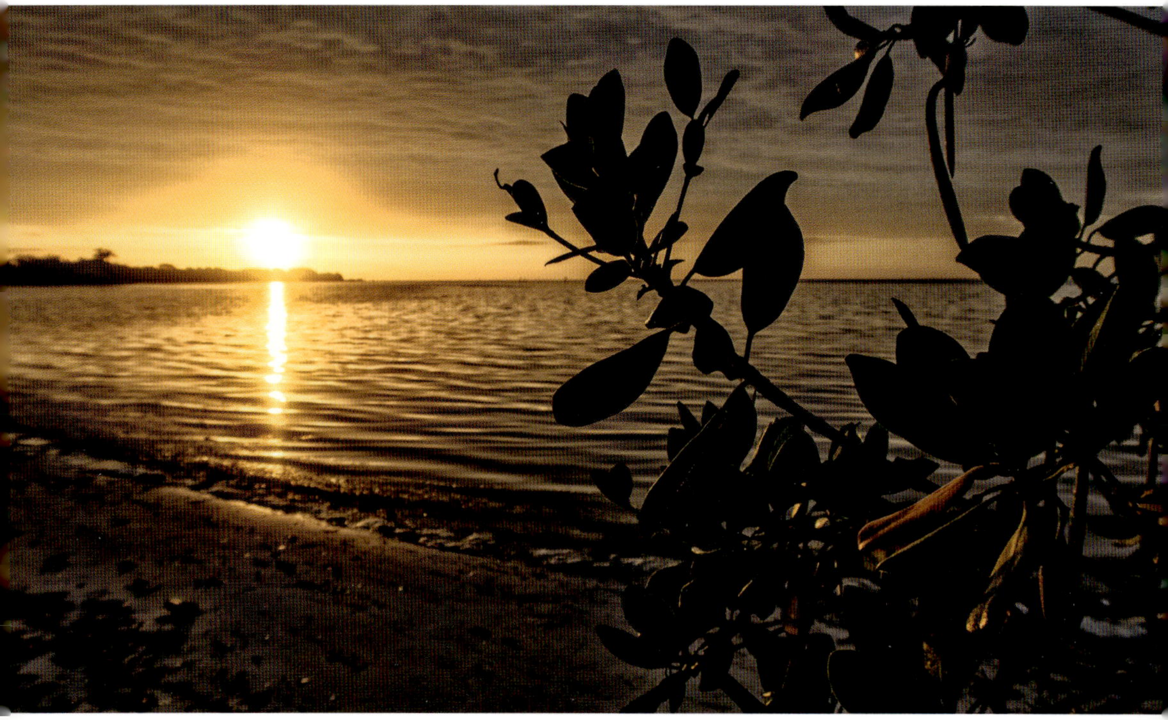

While this is a serious threat to the survival of mangroves in their current range, there is some silver lining for these magnificent trees in the broader story of climate change.

Mangroves are extremely sensitive to frost—but as average global temperatures rise, the mangrove's preferred subtropical climate zone is extending northward. This process is measurable on an alarmingly short timescale.

Case in point: Merritt Island National Wildlife Refuge, near Kennedy Space Center sits at the north edge of mangroves' historic range. But beginning in the late 2010s, as temperatures rose, the area saw a 70-percent increase—a veritable explosion—in its mangrove population, replacing zones previously characterized as salt marshes.[4]

Similar phenomena have been reported as far north as St. Augustine and the Florida Panhandle. Both regions have traditionally been on the tenuous margins of mangrove habitation—cold snaps keep the population in check. But as frosts have become fewer and further between over the last decade, mangroves are moving in.

Mangroves are well-suited to take advantage of shifting climate zones.

As the torpedo-like propagules of red mangroves drop into coastal waters, they have been known to disperse up to 1,000 miles on the currents of the vast ocean before finally coming to rest. They are likely to continue colonizing warmer, newly hospitable coastlines farther north.

That is, if oceanfront development in north Florida and farther up the U.S. coastline has not already boxed them out of these potential homes.

The mangroves strike back, you could say, with some half-hearted degree of conviction. If we give them space to rally.

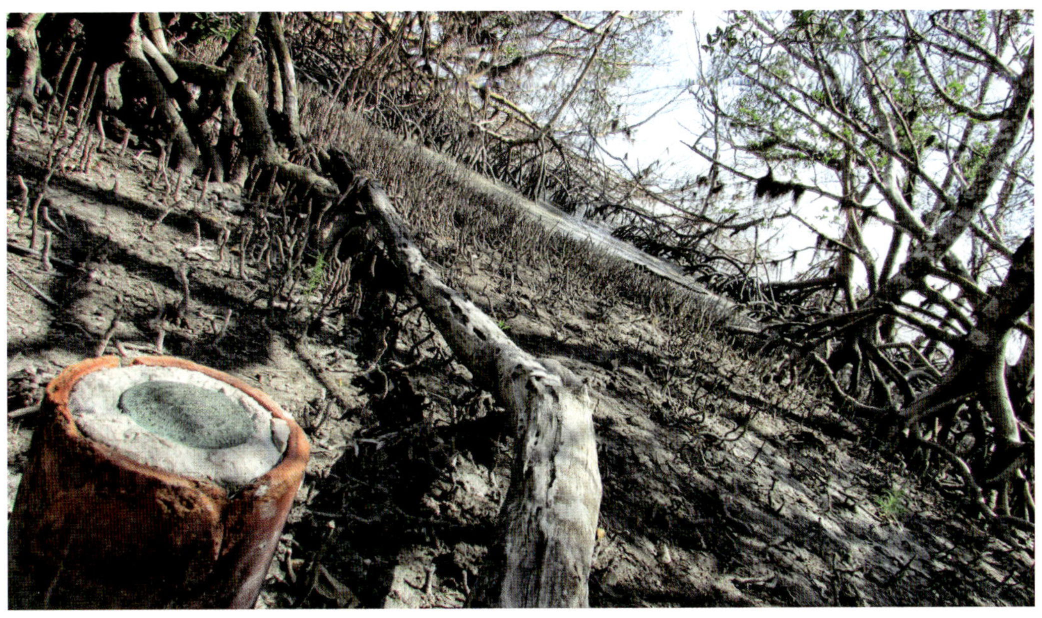

These mangroves near Flamingo in Everglades National Park took a hard blow from Hurricane Irma in 2017. Research suggests that substantial storm surge in the area may have deposited more than an inch of soil onto the floor of the ruined forest, better preparing the trees that take their place to withstand rising sea levels.

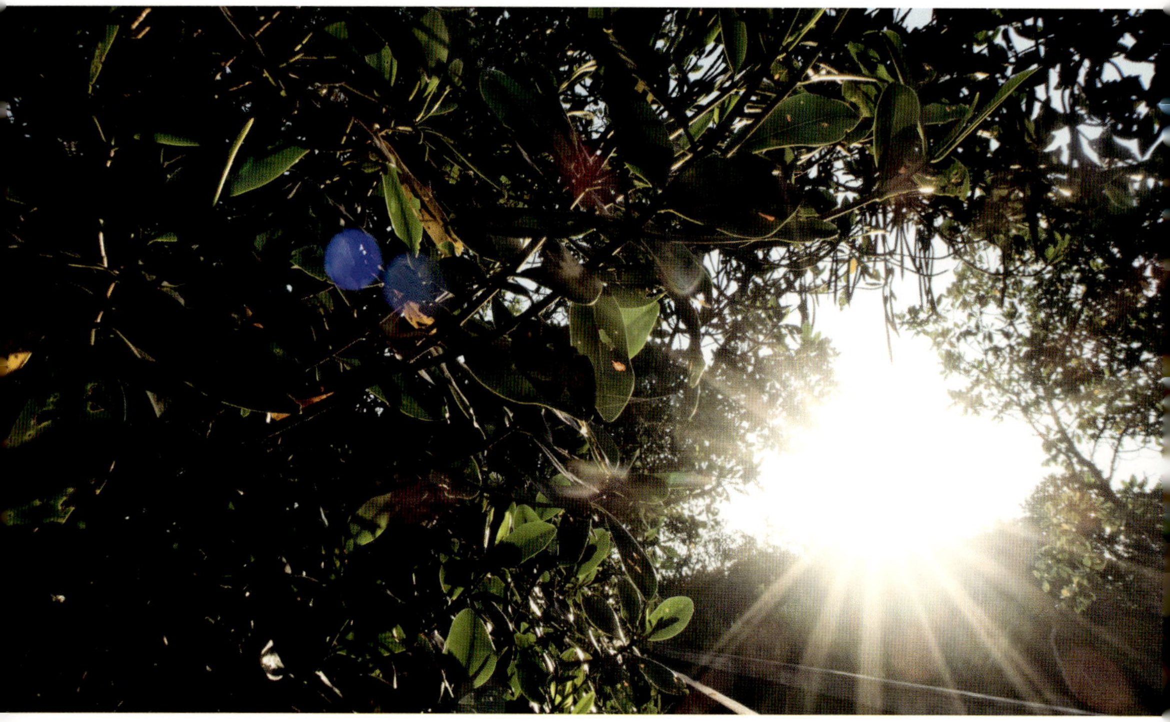

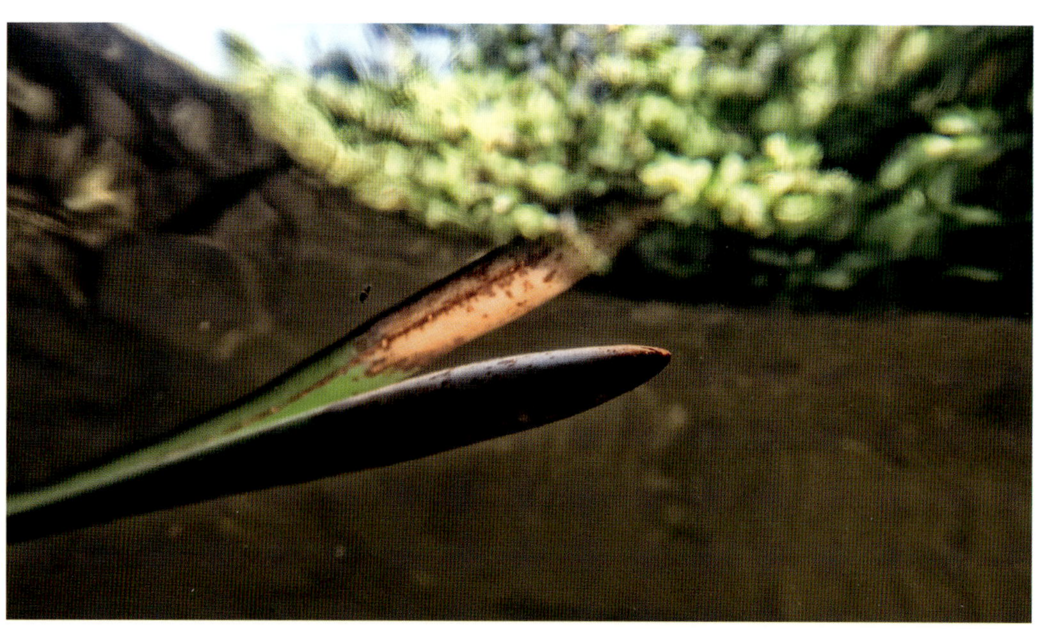

A red mangrove propagule floats just beneath the water's surface. This resilient propagule will remain viable for as long as a year. It may drift a few feet or thousands of miles before coming to rest, depending on the currents and the tides.

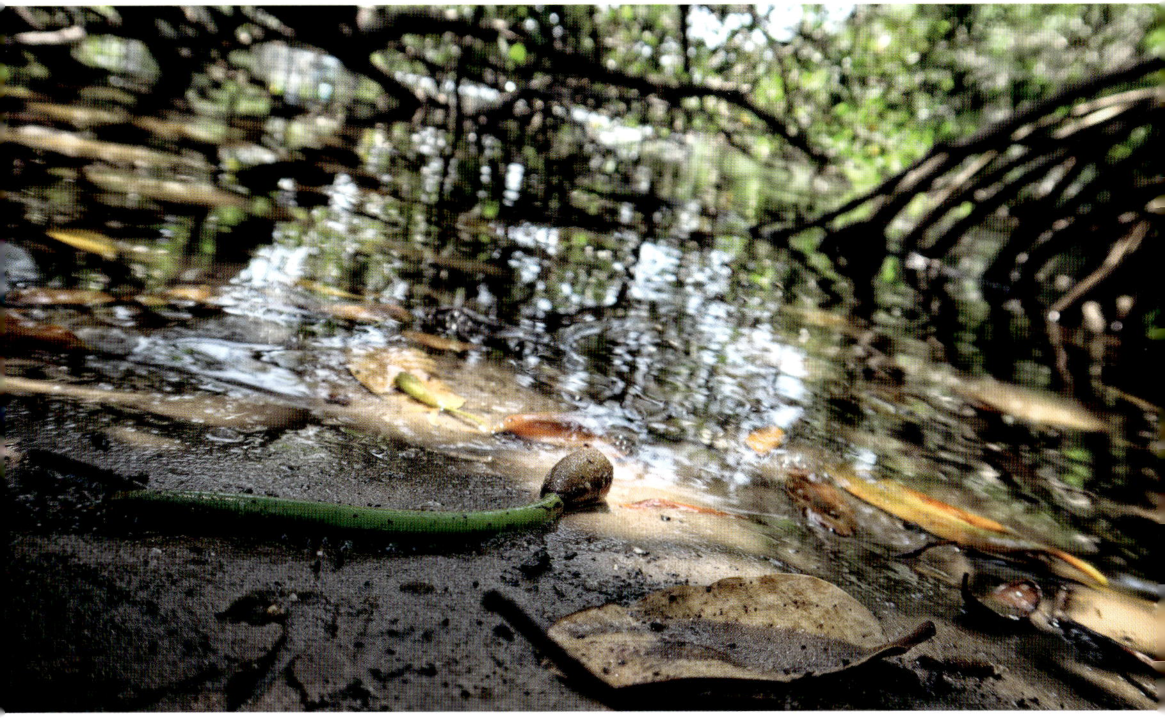

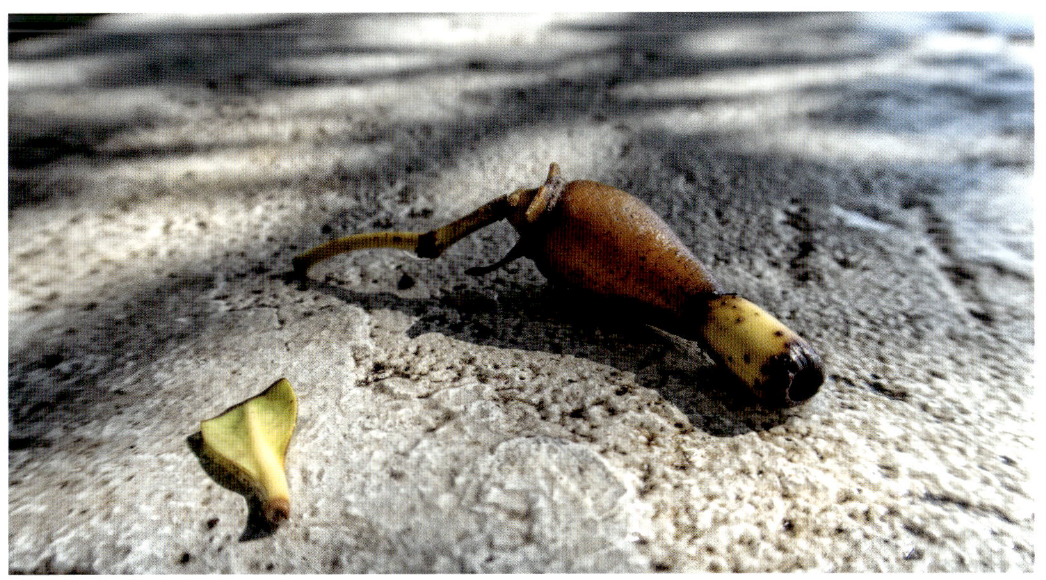

This mangrove propagule has come to rest on the water's edge, perhaps to expand the species' bulwark against the sea.

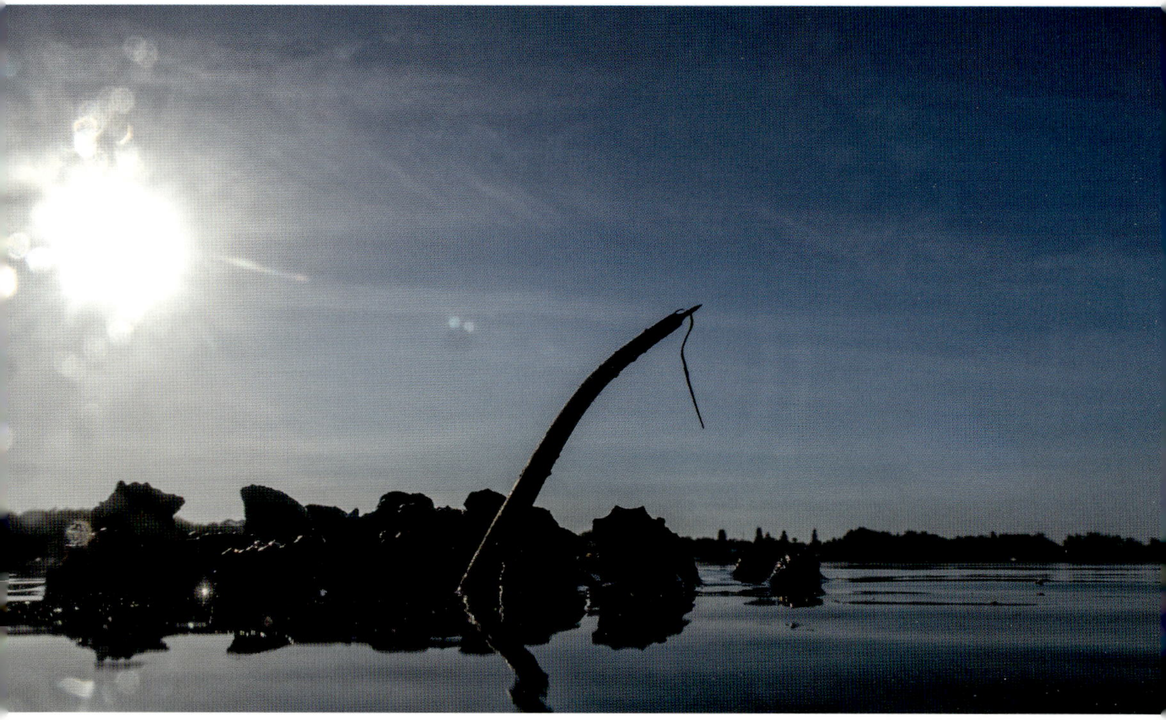

A red mangrove propagule, wedged firmly into an oyster reef.

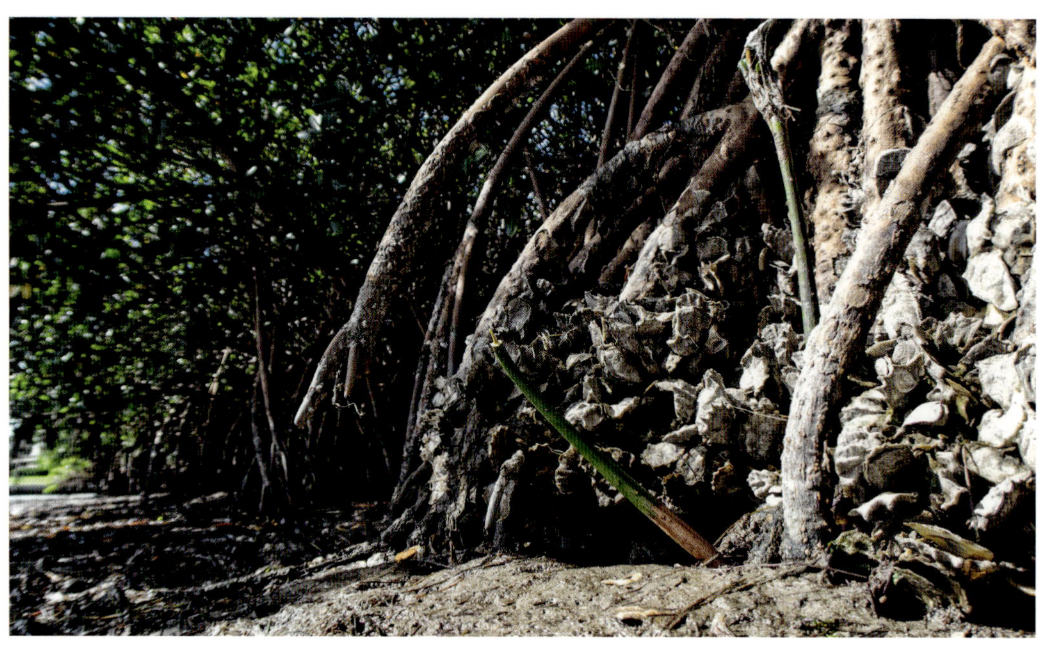

A red mangrove propagule, ready to make a go of it in the rich soils of an established forest.

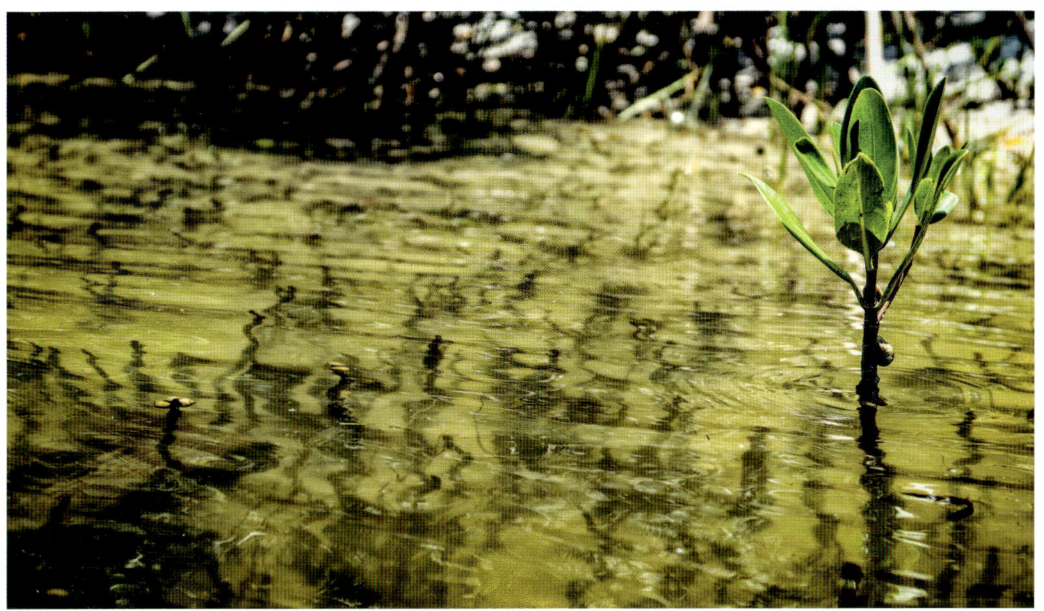

Aquatic snails cling to a young tree, surrounded by a veritable jungle of submerged black mangrove pneumatophores.

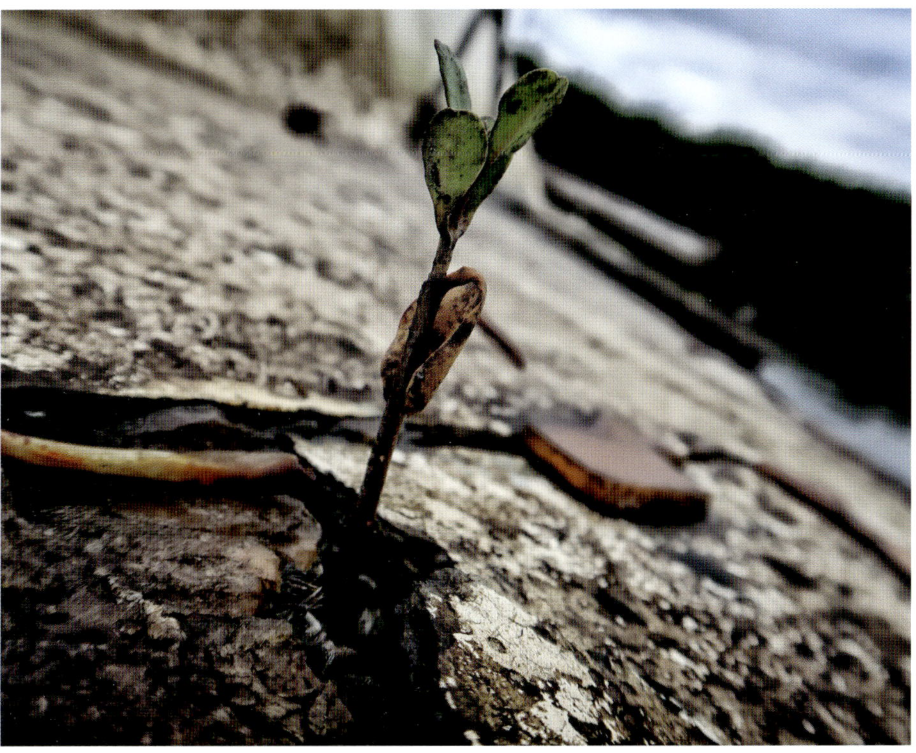

A red mangrove takes root on the wreck of an abandoned boat.

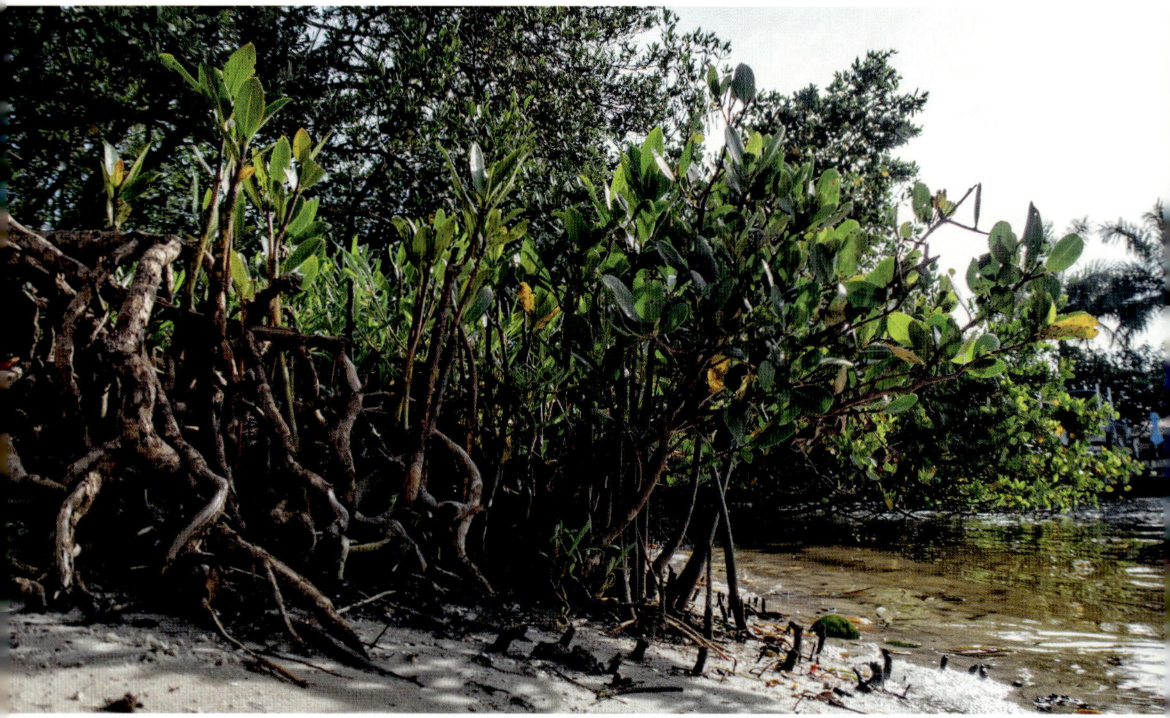

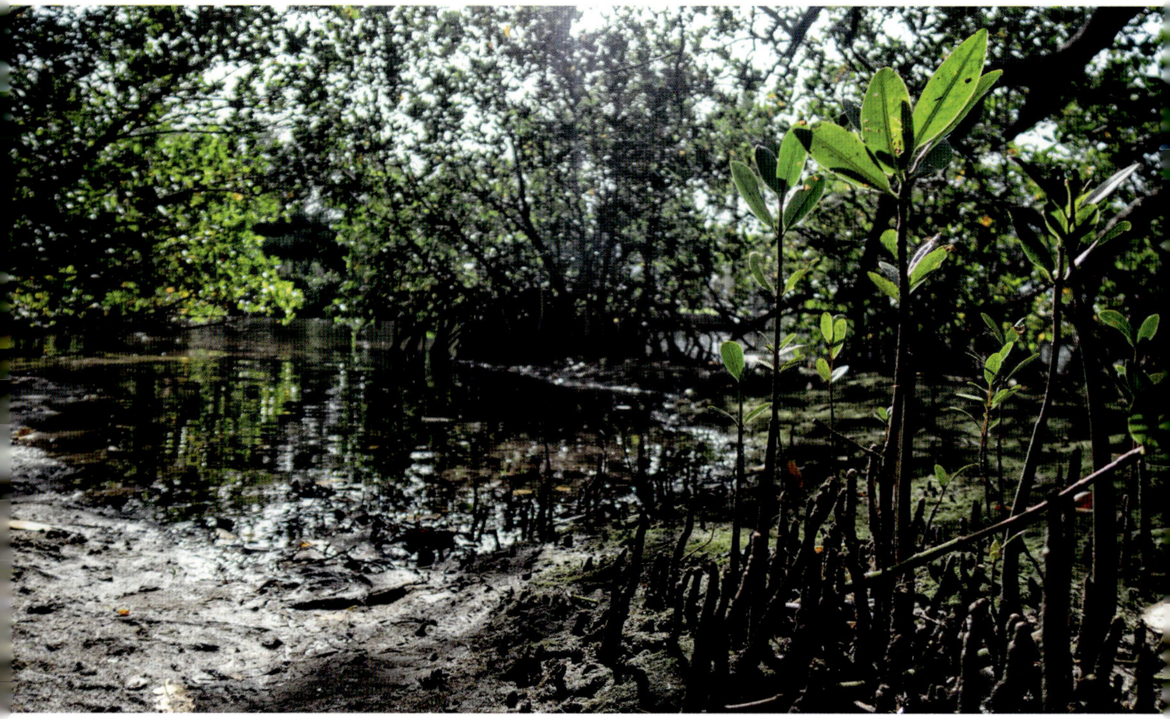

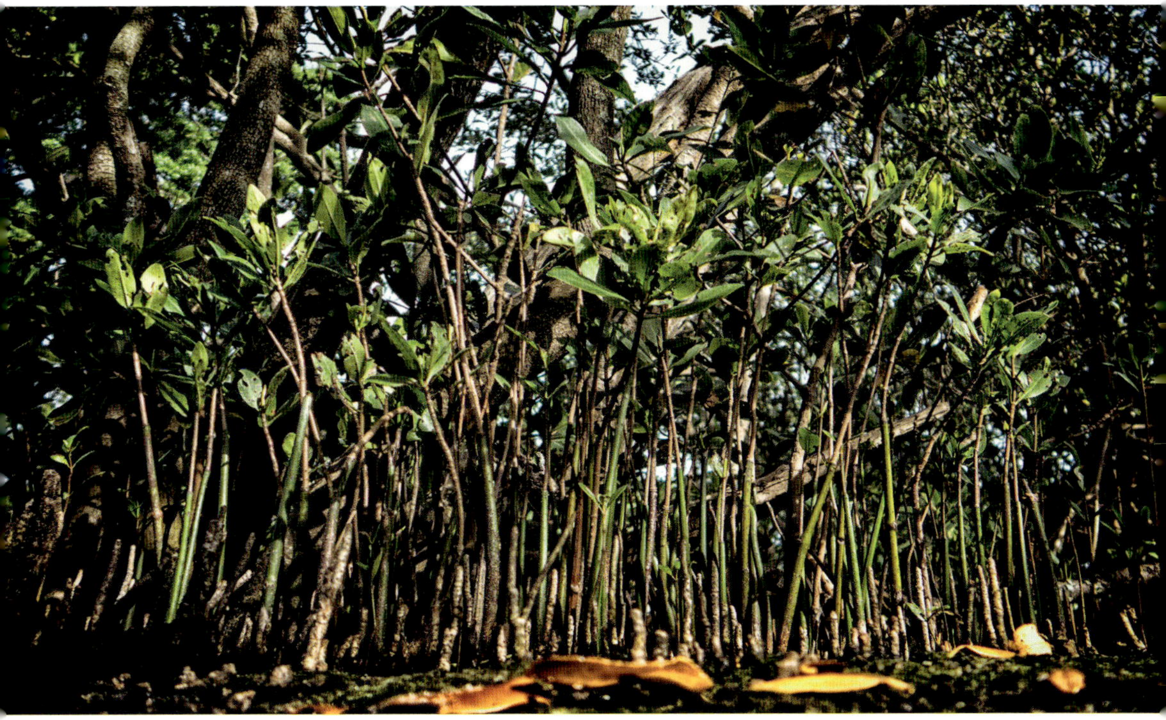

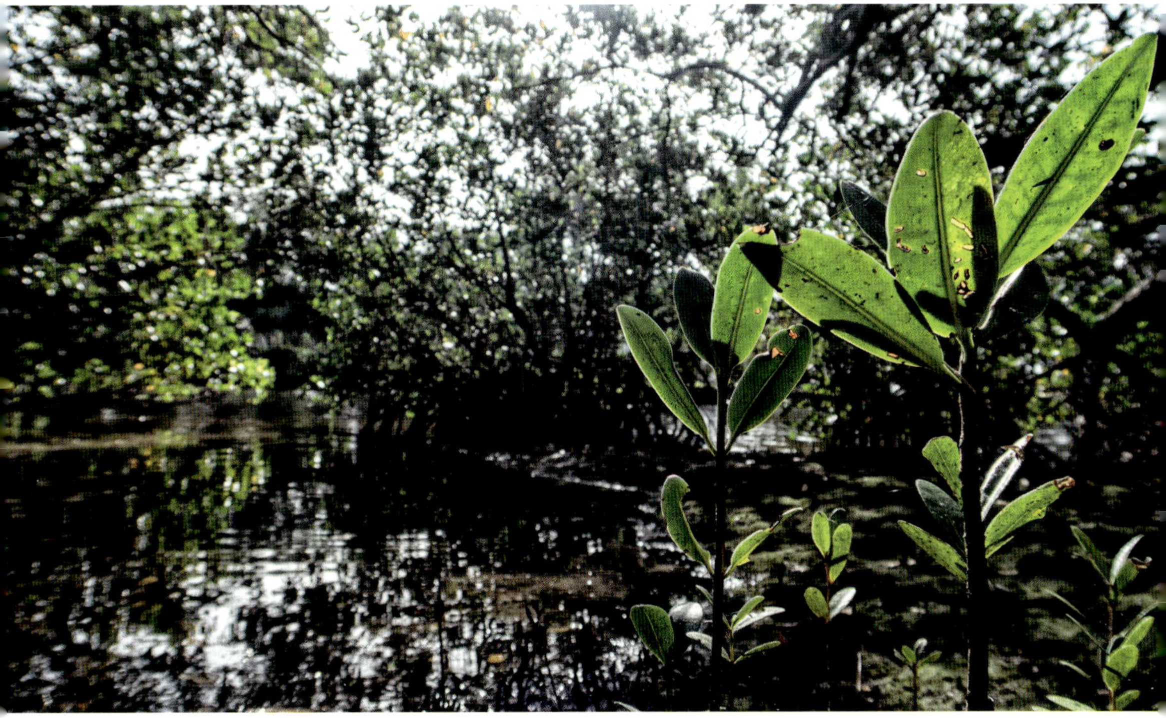

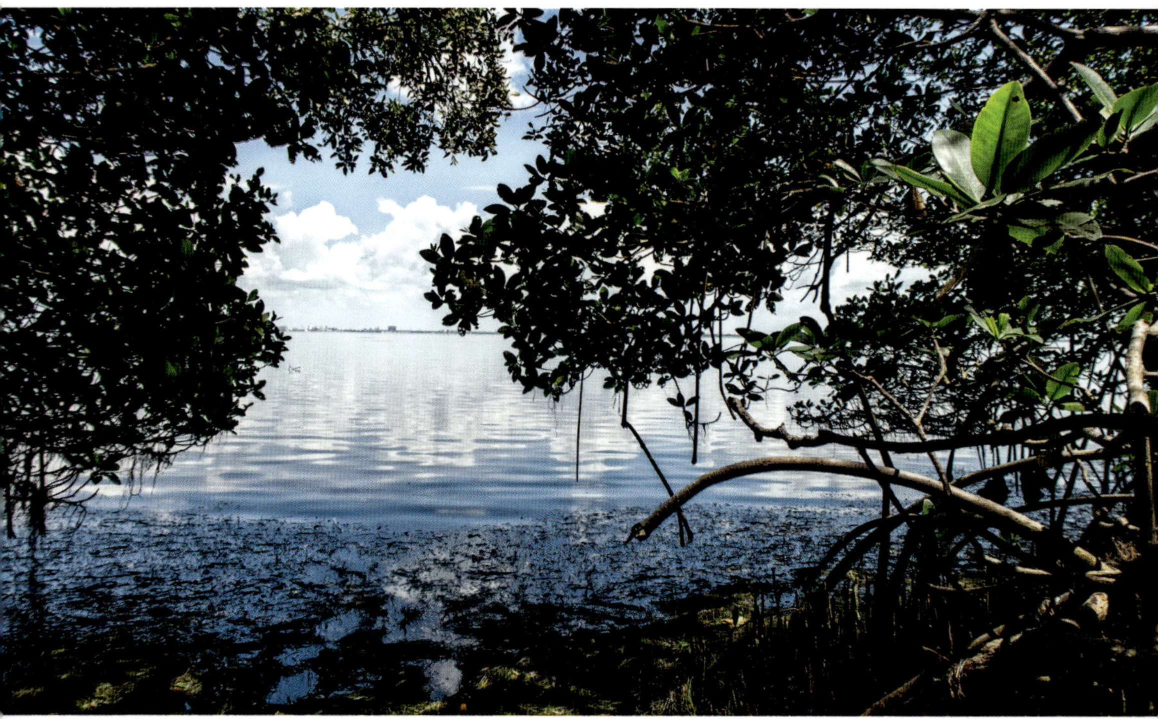

Here's the other upshot: Researchers have demonstrated that mangroves are one of the best carbon sinks in the natural world, storing more than twice as much carbon as much as ten times the carbon as a similar area of terrestrial rainforest forest.[5]

Acre per acre, mangroves "are the world champions of carbon sequestration," ecologist Neil Saintilan told the *Washington Post* in 2020.[6]

This is because of the unique way in which these "blue forests" lock that carbon away. The silty, meters-deep soil in which mangroves flourish—that muck in which your kayak drags at low tide—imprisons tremendous amounts of organic matter shed from above. Dead leaves, smothered propagules, animal droppings, and more are deposited, layer after layer, trapped amidst the spidery legs of the mangroves, falling at a rate far too great for the fungi, bacteria, and invertebrates that populate the forest floor to consume entirely. This deep morass is packed densely, pickled in a fairly anaerobic brine—basically beyond the reach of even the most enthusiastic decomposers above.

And so, a lot of that matter remains, sequestered as successive strata are laid on top. In a healthy mangrove forest, the carbon dioxide and methane that would otherwise be released from decomposition might instead be stored for millennia.[7]

The emphasis here, of course, is that this is what happens in a healthy swamp. As we have established, Florida's track record of maintaining healthy mangrove habitats is not great. While healthy mangroves alone will not save the planet from the worst effects of climate change, restoring and expanding their current range could be a meaningful victory in humanity's struggle to stabilize the worldwide climate system at a time when we need all hands on deck.

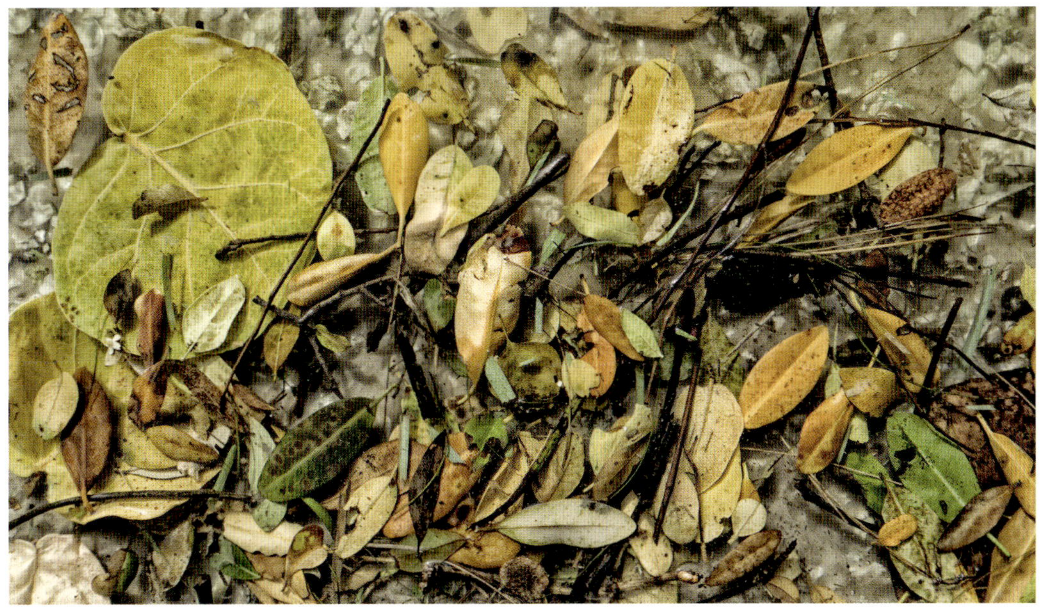

Detritus collecting on the forest floor; carbon captured from the atmosphere.

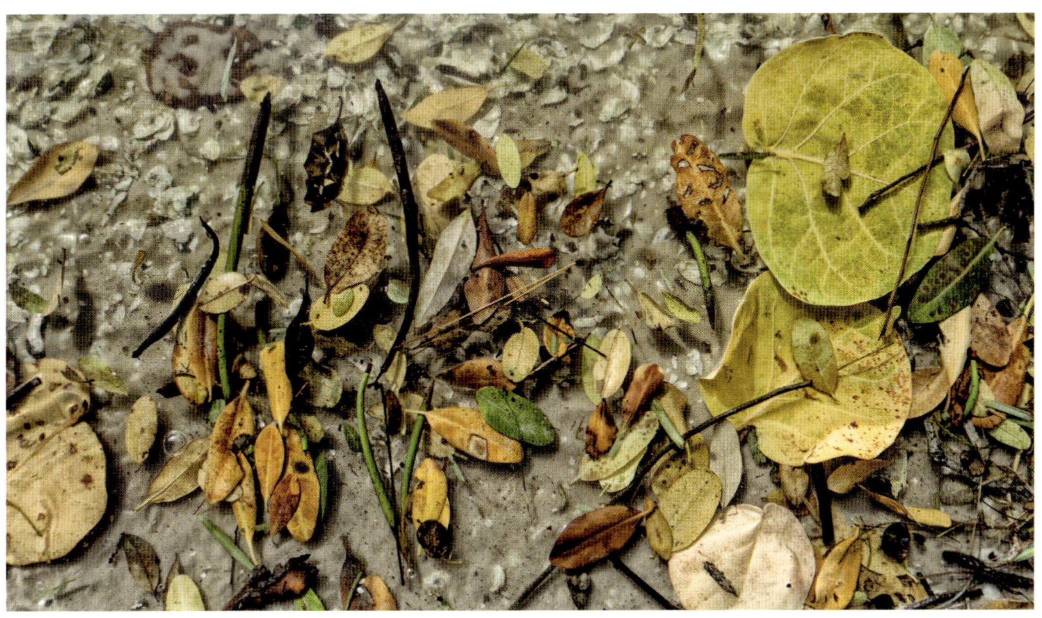

Some small percentage will make it out to sea, but most will be trapped in the prop roots and pneumatophores before it is digested by the diverse decomposing denizens of the mangrove forest—the fungi, the mangrove crabs, and others who will convert this mélange into its base nutrients.

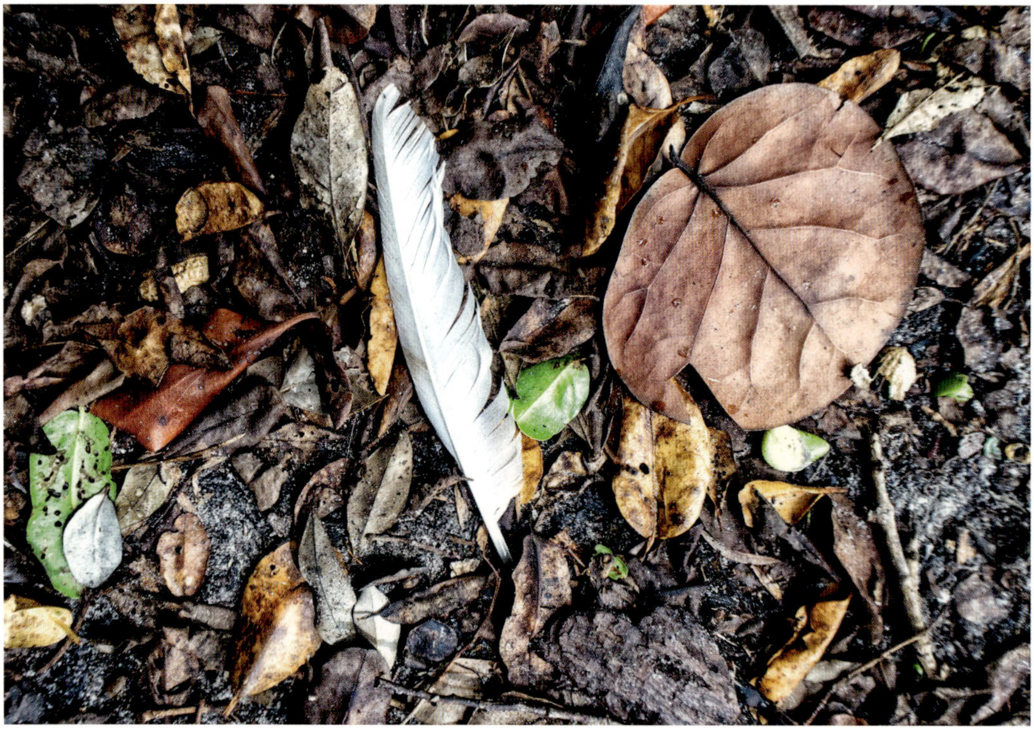

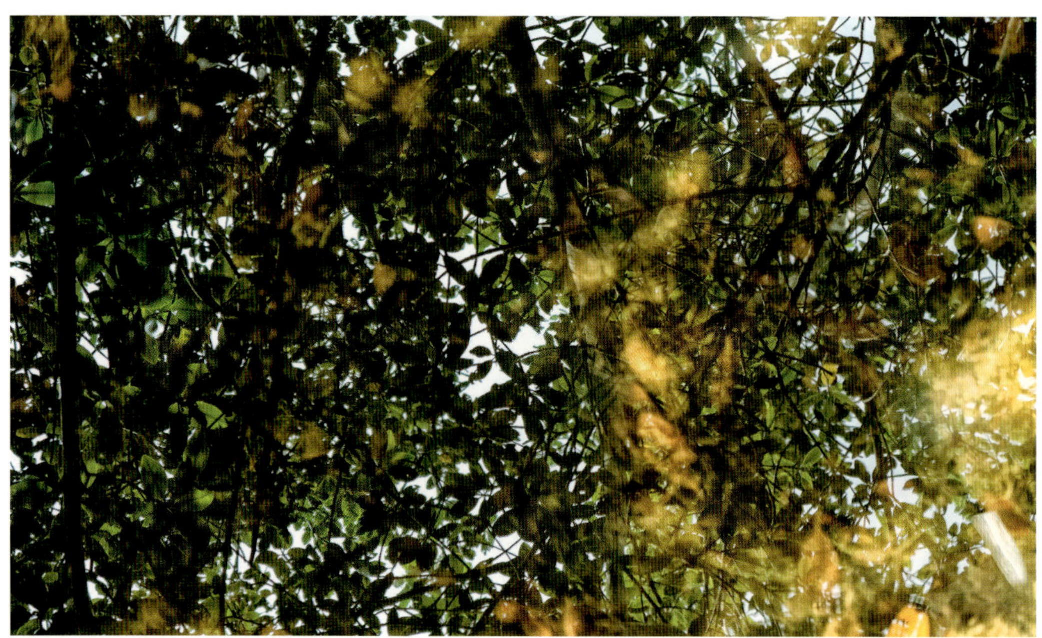

If Monet painted Florida—reflections on a flooded mangrove forest floor, high tide.

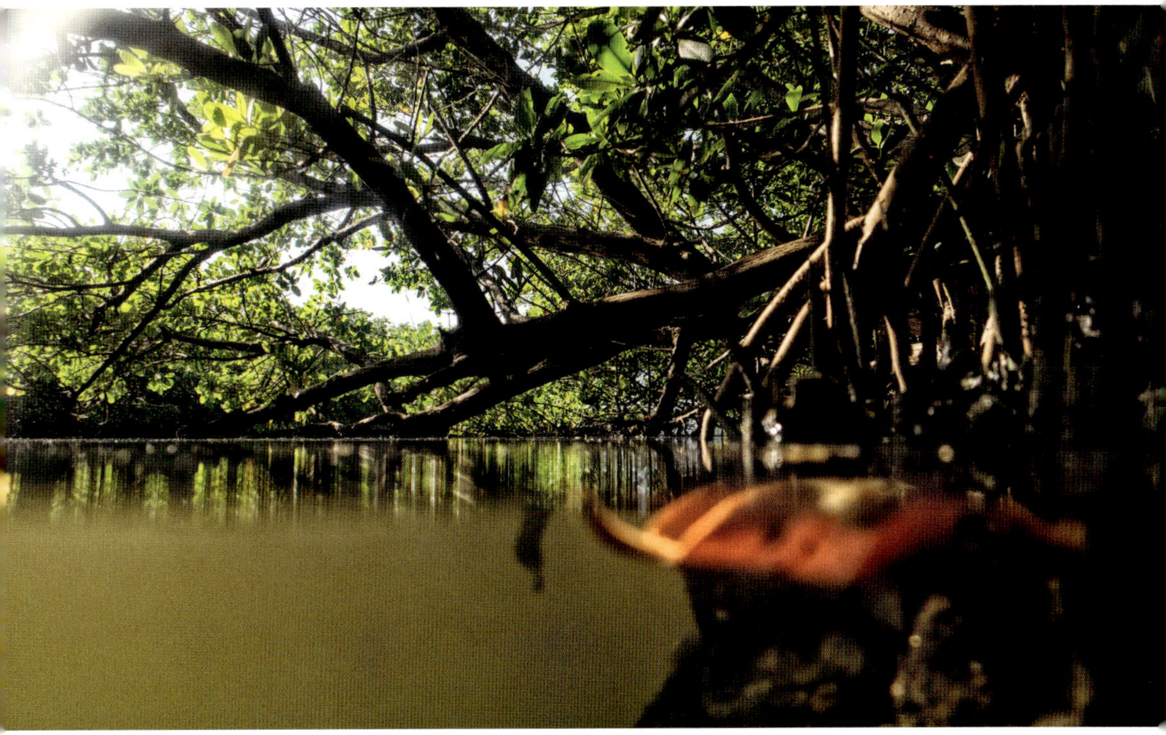

A salty yellow leaf has been cast off.

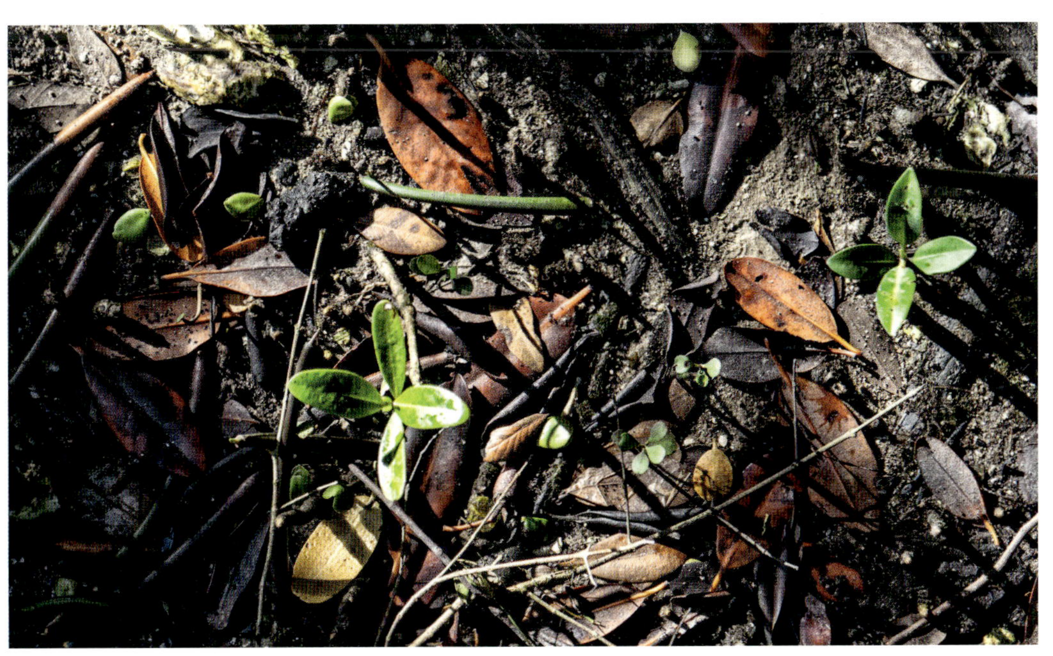

New growth emerges from old as the forest ecosystem perpetuates itself.

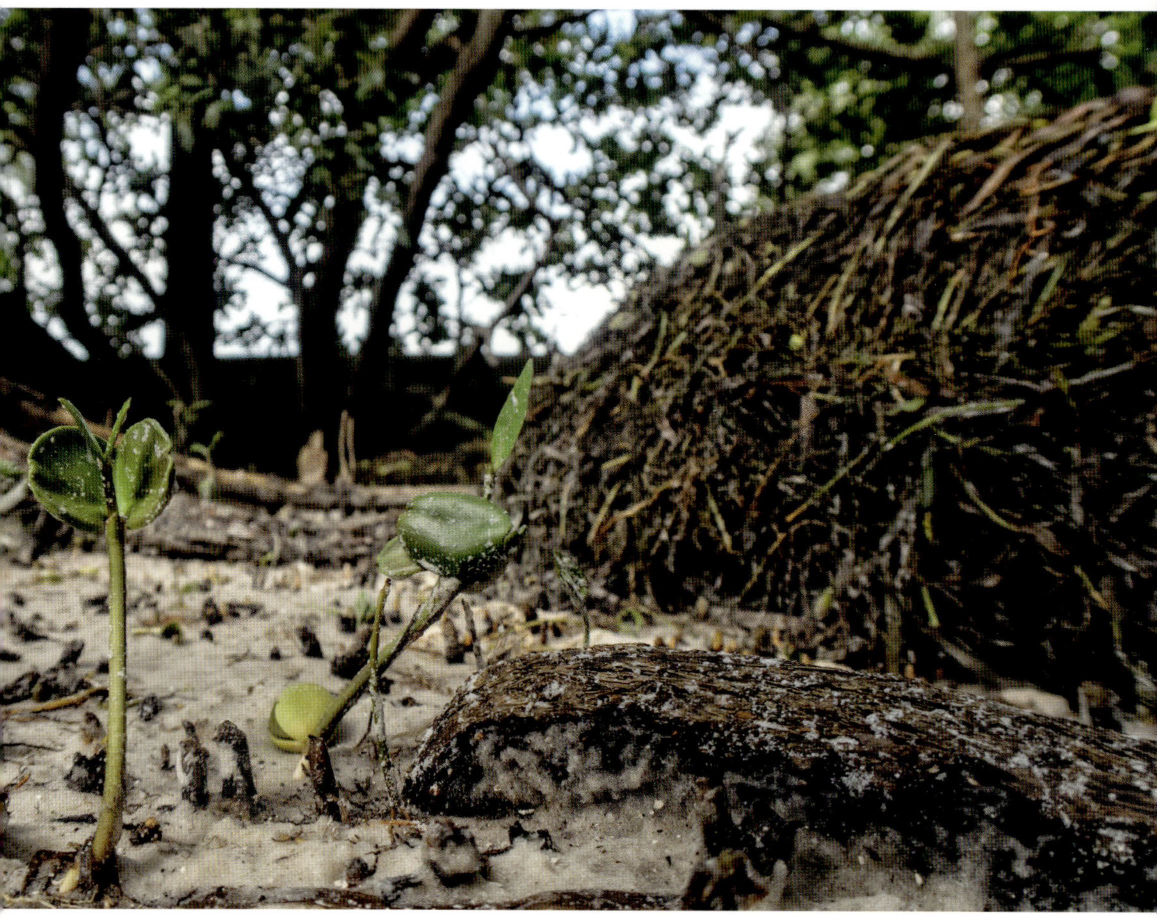

Mangroves sprout amid a shag carpet of seagrass, propagules, and other debris trapped by the prop roots and pneumatophores of an emergent mangrove forest. This is one small step by which mangroves facilitate the creation of new land from the sea—and a small cause for some hope in the era of climate catastrophe.

Our collective back is up against the seawall—and it is my understanding that against the wall is not a strictly desirably place to be.

But the bleakness of the situation makes for a good rallying cry, at least: Tear down the seawall.

Bring on the mangroves.

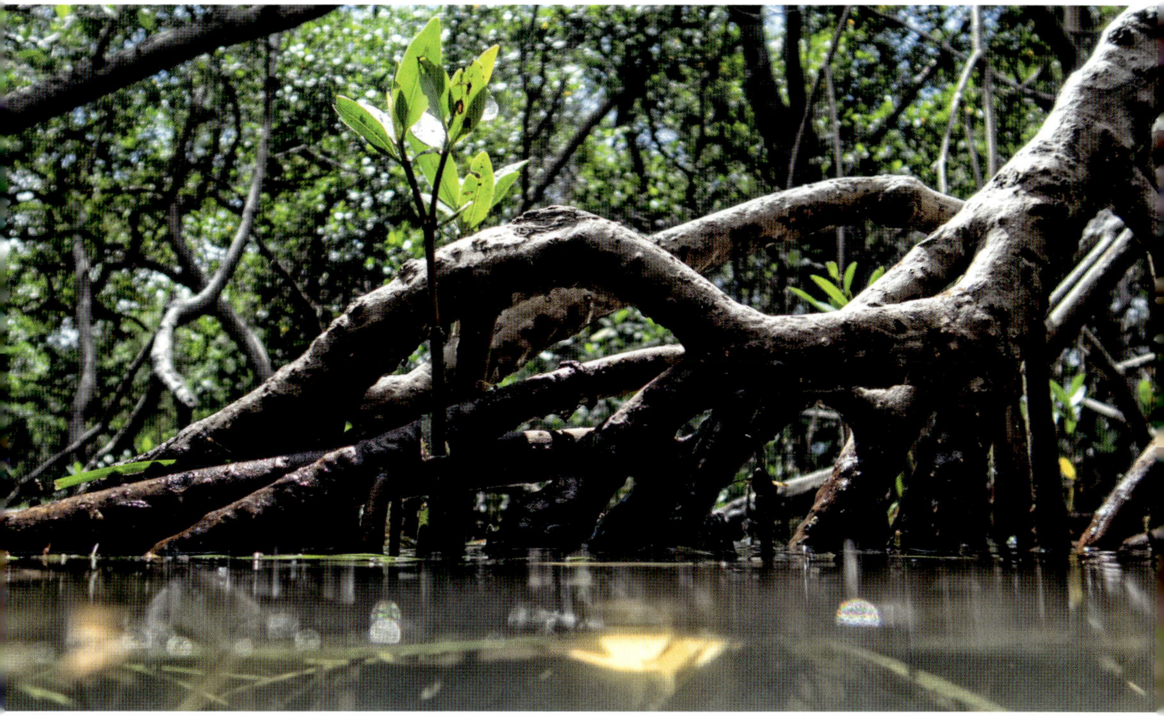

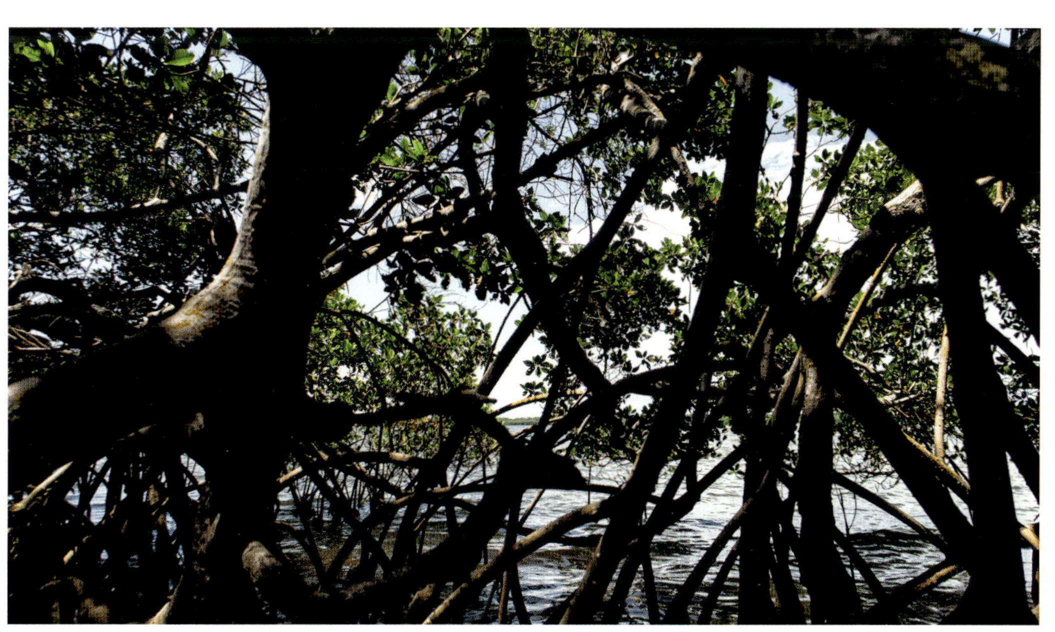

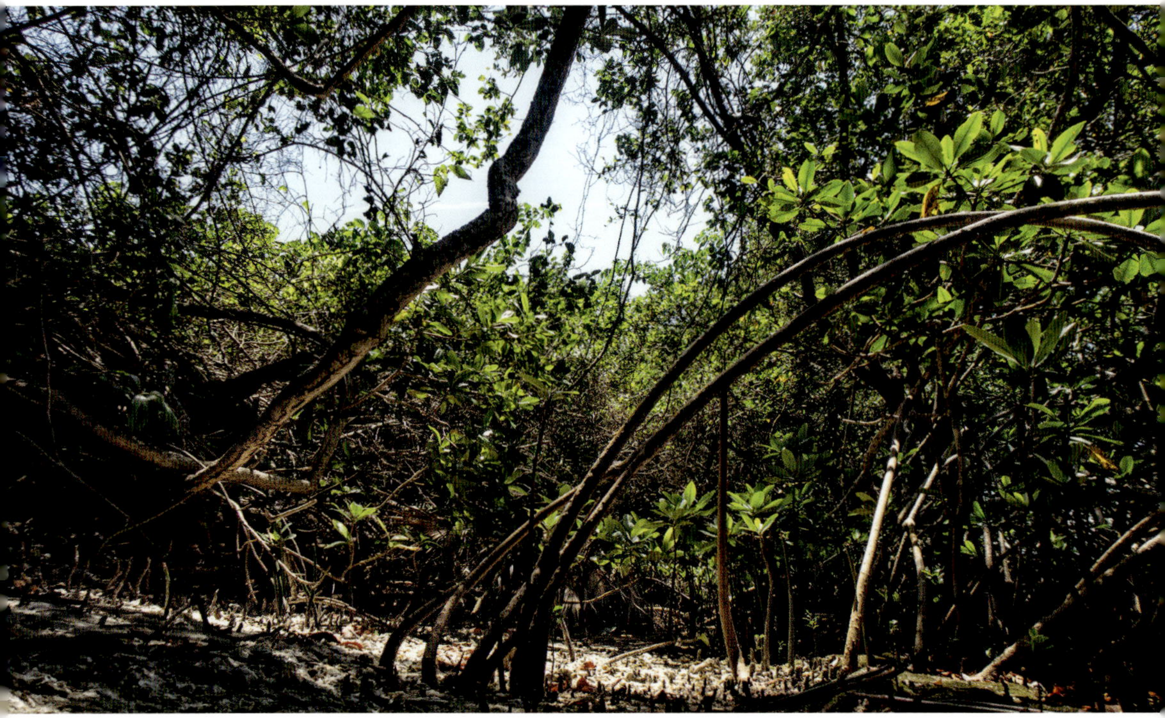

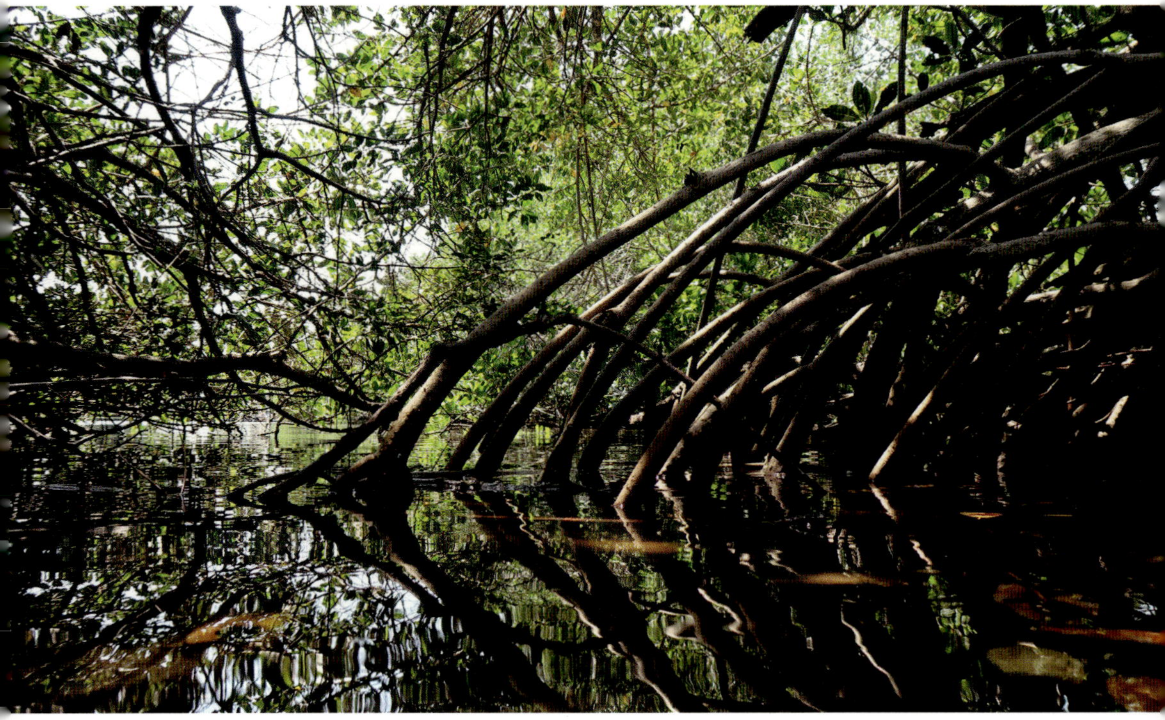

EPILOGUE

The ancient Chinese invented a form of torture known as "death by a thousand cuts," the key characteristic of which is, that while a victim is slashed a multitude of times, no one laceration on the body of the condemned is lethal. No single cut kills. All the same, the end result of death by a thousand cuts is right there in the name—a long, slow, unimaginably painful execution.

I humbly submit that we Floridians have perfected this process writ large, on the very land we profess to love.

If that sentiment seems too harsh, go stand in the middle of any golf course—a vast monoculture of grass, inhospitable to any living thing except human beings with money. A swath of land requiring insane amounts of upkeep—because it is not a natural occurrence in the world. Imagine something like the Ten Thousand Islands in its place, teeming with life unquantifiable, sequestering carbon instead of emitting it—a splendid jade gleaming in the Florida sun.

And then, tell me truthfully that the land has not been slashed—cut to the bone.

It bears writing down—I am not anti-golf, anti-housing, or anti-anything, really, except the thought that we can march on indefinitely as if development were largely a question of economics, a matter of supply and demand, of personal liberty—with no repercussions that cannot be mitigated by paying a fine or planting two trees elsewhere on the property.

You are not the problem. I am not the problem.

No single housing development, no one stretch of seawall, no individual theme park or golf course is to blame. Each on its own is all fine and well and good.

And yet taken together, Floridians have on their hands a collective problem that requires collective action to redress.

If all of this seems immoderate, it is only because the mainstream national discourse about the environment is itself so extreme—tilted against the rights of nature, against cooperation, and too often for a brand of the American dream that promotes consumption as a stand in for citizenship. I posit a new American value—not bigger, not more, but enough.

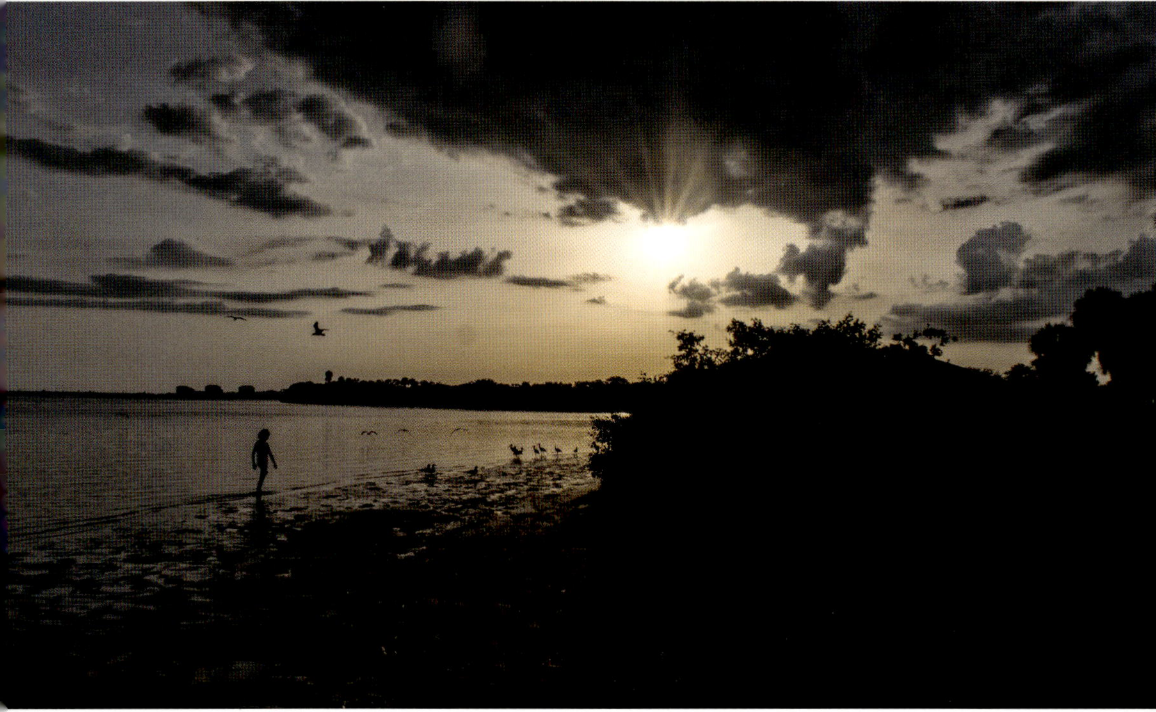

As the storm clears—a Florida we can be proud to pass on to the next generation.

Enough for everyone, man, beast, or mangrove.

The economy is important, yes, but so is the sustainability of life as we know it on this planet. There must be a balance, and I am not sure that we have achieved it yet—globally, nationally, or locally. Mangroves are just one indicator of this larger concern, and I do not mean to suggest they are a panacea for all of our environmental woes. But the fact is, whether it is piecemeal or wholesale, whole hog or just this once because the developer is a major campaign contributor: We are pulling this state apart one acre at a time, rending it by force until it breaks.

In the era of climate crisis, we must adapt, or we will fail to thrive.

We must think harder about the rights of nature.

We need to be thoughtful about how we manage our resources. We must be wary of pricing the land in dollars and cents, as if there will always be another patch of the natural world to pave over with little regard to the broader consequences. As if the fate of humanity were not closely tied to the health of everything else around us.

As if, because our forerunners "saved the Everglades," our conservation work in the state of Florida was done.

No biome is expendable. Yet there are few that Floridians abuse at their own peril more so than the mangroves.

Climate change can seem like an intractable, impossibly global problem. But the truth is, it is a challenge that will be met through countless small actions taken in communities

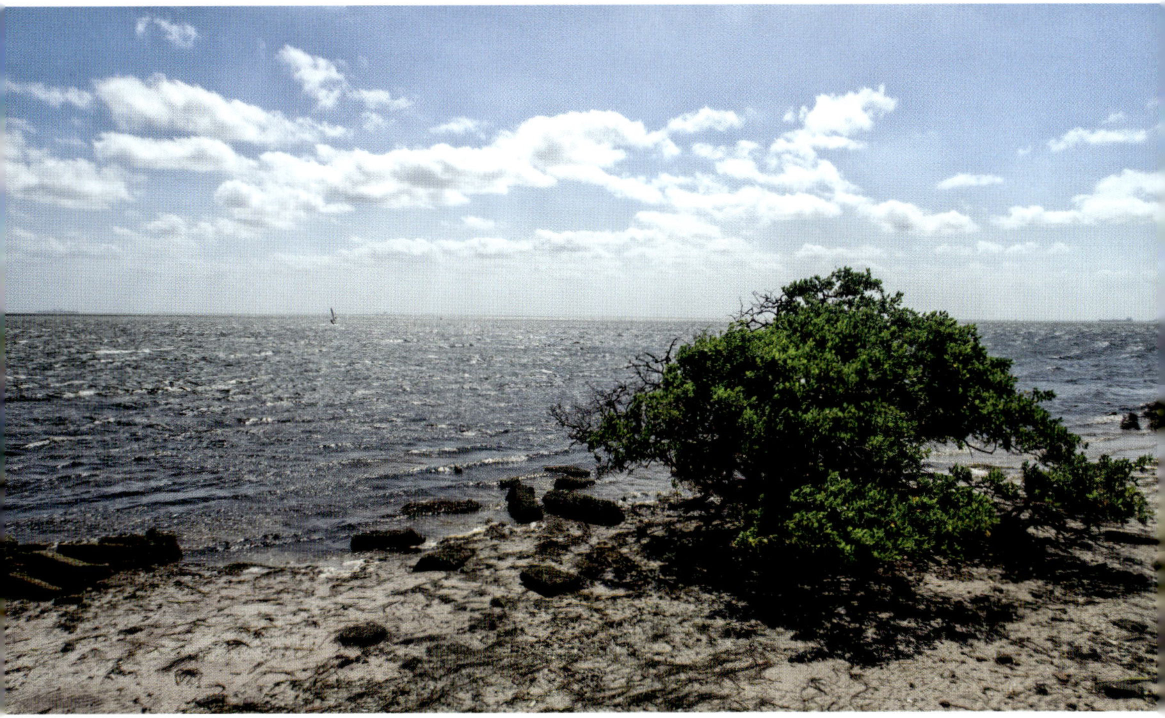

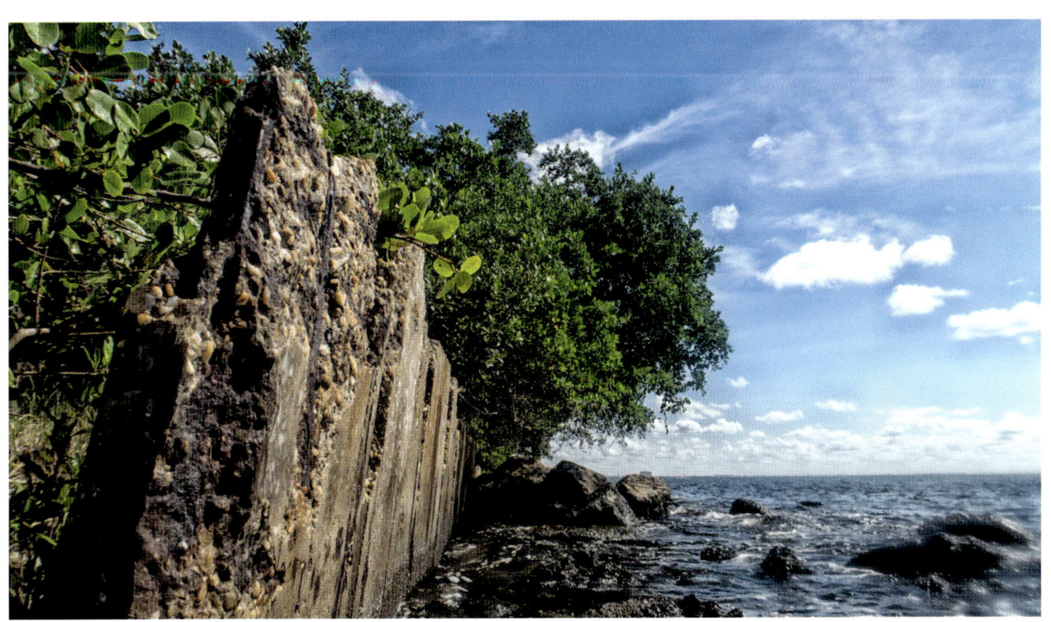

May many other seawalls meet a similar fate.

just like ours. And better stewardship of natural Florida, beginning with the mangroves, is one of the single most powerful contributions that Floridians can make toward that common cause.

Just as no one of us is to blame for this monumental problem, no one of us can resolve it either. But we can start to think hard about whether we want to be part of the problem—or part of the solution.

I am, to the core, an optimist. It is why I just wrote this mushy love letter to the mangroves. I suspect you are right there with me, since you have read this far.

I see a path forward for the mangroves—and for man.

Together, in a mutually beneficial union.

What do you say—are you Team Mangrove, too?

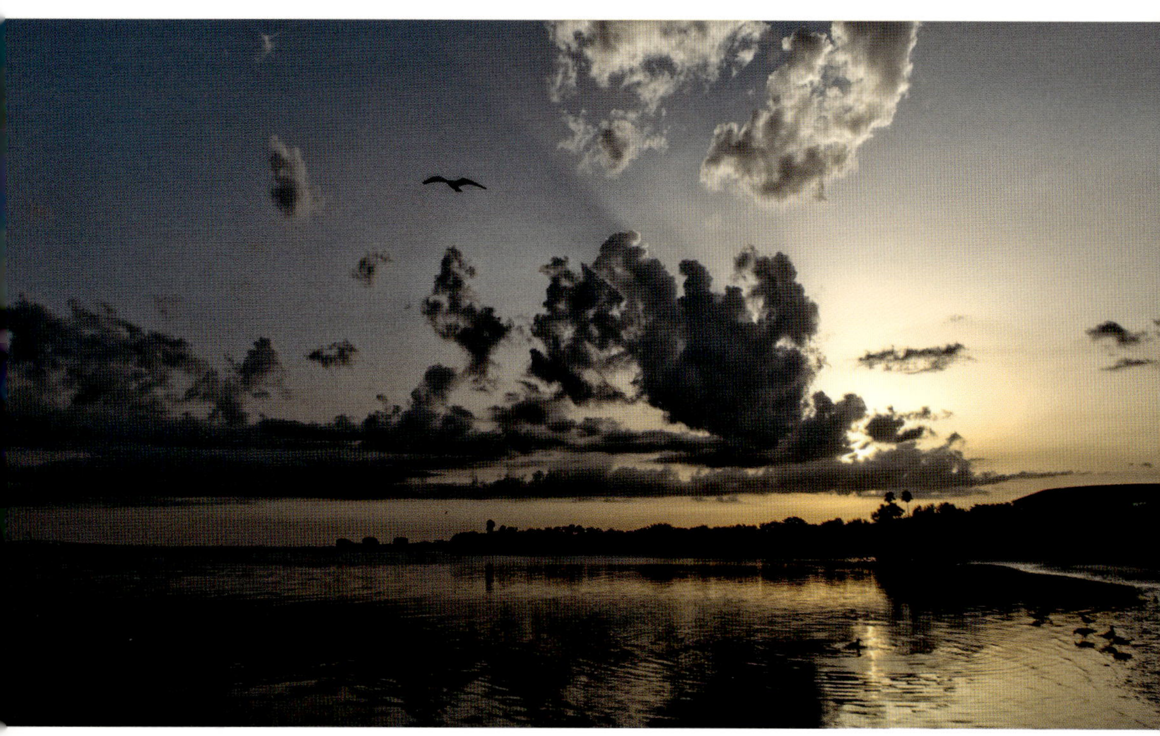

ENDNOTES

CHAPTER 1

1 Blankespoor, B., Dasgupta, S., Lange, G., (2017). "Mangroves as a protection from storm surges in a changing climate." *Ambio*, 46, 478-491.

2 Doughty, C. L., Cavanaugh, K. C., Hall, C. R., *et al.*, (2017). "Impacts of mangrove encroachment and mosquito impoundment management on coastal protection services." *Hydrobiologia* 803, 105–120.

3 Danielsen, F., Sørensen, M., Olwig, M., Selvam, V., Parish, F., Burgess, N., Hiraishi, T., Karunagaran, V., Rasmussen, M., Hansen, L., Quarto, A., and Suryadiputra, N. (2005). "The Asian Tsunami: A Protective Role for Coastal Vegetation." *Science* (New York, N.Y.). 310.

4 Committee on Commerce, Science, and Transportation, United States Senate, (2017). *Threats Facing Florida's Tourism Driven Economy.*

CHAPTER 2

1 Widmer, R. J., (1988). *The Evolution of Calusa: A Nonagricultural Chiefdom of the Southwest Florida Coast* (University of Alabama Press, Feb. 28, 1988).

2 Thompson, V. D., Marquardt, W. H., Savarese, M., Walker, K. J., Newsom, L. A., Lulewicz, I., Lawres, N. R., Roberts Thompson, A. D., Bacon, A. R., Walser, C. A. (2020). "Ancient engineering of fish capture and storage in southwest Florida." *Proceedings of the National Academy of Sciences* Apr 2020, 117 (15) 8374-8381.

3 Morrero, T. (2015). "Ancient canoe comes to life in display at Weedon Island Preserve." *Tampa Bay Times* Oct. 16, 2015.

4 Horwitz, T. (2008). *A Voyage Long and Strange: Rediscovering the New World. United States* (Henry Holt and Company).

CHAPTER 3

1 Feller, I. "C." (2019). "Climate change pushes Florida's mangroves north." PBS Newshour, March 31, 2019.

2 Arsenault, R. (1996). *St. Petersburg and the Florida Dream, 1888–1950* (United States: University Press of Florida).

3 *Ibid.*

4 *St. Petersburg: An Oral History.* (2002). (United States: Arcadia Pub.).

5   The Editorial Board. (2017) "How Federal Flood Insurance Puts Homes at Risk." *The New York Times*. Aug. 31, 2017.

6   "FACT SHEET: Acquisition of Property After a Flood Event." FEMA. Nov. 13, 2018. www.fema.gov/news-release/2018/11/13/fact-sheet-acquisition-property-after-flood-event Accessed Jul 7, 2020.

7   Freedman, A. "Climate change could cost the US 10.5 percent of GDP by 2100." *The Washington Post*. Aug. 19, 2019.

CHAPTER 4

1   "Mangroves: Multi-Species Recovery Plan for South Florida." Federal Fish and Wildlife Service. 2020.

2   Lewis, R. R., Gilmore, Jr., R. R., Crewz, D. W., and Odum, W. E. 1985. "Mangrove habitat and fishery resources of Florida." Pages 281-336 in "Florida aquatic habitat and fishery resources." W. Seaman, Jr. (ed.), American Fisheries Society.

3   "Mangroves: Multi-Species Recovery Plan for South Florida."

4   Lorenz, J. (2013). "Benthic Habitat: Mangroves." National Oceanic and Atmospheric Administration. Sep. 13, 2013.

5   Fisher, K., 1998. "Man Let 'Em Grow: The State of Florida Mangrove Laws." *The Florida Bar Journal* Vol. 72, No. 5. May 1998.

6   Scheider, K. (2020). "Sea-level rise and onshore development are killing Florida's mangroves. Here's why that matters." *USA Today*. Feb. 14, 2020.

7   Parsons, V. (2014). "'Giant' Restoration is Prototype for Tampa Bay Mangroves." *Bay Soundings*. Jan. 17, 2014.

CHAPTER 5

1   Alongi, D. M. "The Impact of Climate Change on Mangrove Forests." *Curr Clim Change Rep* 1, 30–39 (2015).

2   Saintilan, N., Khan, N. S., Ashe, E., *et al.* "Thresholds of mangrove survival under rapid sea level rise." *Science* (New York, N.Y.). 2020 June; 368(6495):1118-1121.

3   Feller, I. "C." (2019). "Climate change pushes Florida's mangroves north." PBS Newshour, March 31, 2019.

4   Doughty, C. L., Langley, J. A., Walker, W. S., *et al.* "Mangrove Range Expansion Rapidly Increases Coastal Wetland Carbon Storage." *Estuaries and Coasts* 39, 385–396 (2016).

5   *Ibid.*

6   Popkin, G. (2020). "Mangrove loss has fallen dramatically, but the forests are still in danger." *The Washington Post*. Sep. 12, 2020.

7   Donato, D., Kauffman, J., Murdiyarso, D., *et al.* "Mangroves among the most carbon-rich forests in the tropics." *Nature Geoscience* 4, 293–297 (2011).